Escape to God

HOW OUR FAMILY LEFT THE RAT RACE BEHIND
TO SEARCH FOR GENUINE SPIRITUALITY
AND THE SIMPLE LIFE

Jim Hohnberger

WITH

TIM AND JULIE CANUTESON

Pacific Press® Publishing Association
Nampa, Idaho
Oshawa, Ontario, Canada

Edited by Jerry Thomas
Designed by Tim Larson
Cover photo by Johnston H. Richard © FPG International

All texts taken from the King James Version unless otherwise noted.

ISBN 0-8163-1805-0

01 02 03 04 • 4 3 2 1

Contents

Dedication

To all those in this hour of earth's history whose religious lives are marked by a growing hunger and thirst after God Himself and will not be satisfied until they have learned to daily walk with their Master.

Note:

The stories contained in the following pages are true. They relate to real places and real people and sometimes, where the story mentioned does not reflect poorly upon an individual, I have used their real names. In other cases, the names and unimportant characteristics have been altered to protect the privacy of the individuals. Some events have been shortened for the sake of clarity and brevity. The events however, are true and should any of those concerned read the stories they will see a clear reflection of what happened and truths that can be learned from it.

Preface

"Jim, you really need to put these messages into a book," Jack and his wife, Judy urged.

The thought of such a thing took me by surprise. After all, it was easy for Jack to suggest writing a book. He was a writer. It was second nature for him. English was the one subject in school in which I learned only what was absolutely necessary to get through and then promptly forgot it all.

Me? Write a book? Preposterous! I thanked them, but dismissed the idea. My gifts and abilities definitely lay in verbal communication, not writing. But the idea wouldn't go away. Everywhere I turned, it seemed that friends and acquaintances kept telling me I needed to write a book. Even the letters we received rang with the persistent echo.

At last I decided that maybe God was trying to tell me something. I went to my knees in prayer and asked almost incredulously, "Lord, do You really want *me* to write a book?" When the clear impression in my thoughts was, *Yes Jim, I do,* I was bowled over, astonished, and shocked. "But, I can't do that Lord. I don't have the talent. Above all else, I don't have the time! Due to ministry commitments, my life is planned twelve to eighteen months in advance. I just don't know how I can do it, Lord!"

I tried to put the idea aside, on the back burner so to speak, but it kept coming up in my thoughts again and again. I had already seen how several people had been used of God to give me the idea to write and I knew that the use of multiple people and multiple talents is one of God's most common methods for the accomplishment of His work.

You see, when God calls a man to a task, it is usually a man who is unqualified for the work. That way, the man must be dependent upon God if it is to happen. The temptation for all of us is to take to ourselves the glory, to take the credit for that which God Himself has accomplished. Solomon oversaw the building of the temple at Jerusalem. It was an awesome task involving tens of thousands of workers, and yet he addressed God at the dedication of the structure saying, "this house which I have built is called by Thy name."

Solomon had taken the credit for that which God had done through thousands of workers and the temple would not be called by God's name. Even to this day when that magnificent edifice is mentioned, it is known as Solomon's temple. I didn't want to take the glory for writing a book either. More to the point, I couldn't take the glory for I knew that apart from God's intervention, I couldn't accomplish it.

At last I told the Lord that if He wanted me to write a book then I wanted someone else to tell me. This time I wanted someone different than the well-educated, articulate people who had approached me about writing. "Lord, I want the most humble instrument You can find. If You speak through someone like this, then I will pursue writing a book."

During the fall of 1995, I arrived for a series of meetings in California. The kind people who picked me up from the airport told me about Eleanor. She was just a poor elderly woman who was near death in a nursing home, but she really loved my messages and had experienced a peace with God she had never known prior to hearing my sermons. With this background they shared, "Jim, she is too sick to attend the meetings, but she has expressed a desire to see you. It would mean so very much to her if you would stop in to see her, if only for a few minutes."

After confirming that we had sufficient time in the schedule and praying about the situation, I felt the impression that I should go and see Eleanor. So, we headed to the nursing home. I can't fully describe my feelings as I walked into the room and this woman I had never met exclaimed, "Jim Hohnberger! I don't believe it! Come on over here!" Then she continued. "The Lord told me that you're supposed to write a book." She gestured over to a shelf where several of my tape sets rested and said, "You've got to put all these in a book.

Please Jim, promise me that you'll put these into a book. It's so important for us to have these in book form. Please promise me you'll do it!"

My voice was all choked up and tears filled my eyes because I knew I stood on holy ground. That dying woman had been the instrument chosen by God to push me into action. It was September 8, 1995.

"Eleanor, you are an answer to prayer," I managed to tell her. Eleanor had felt it would be a blessing to meet me, even if only for a few minutes, but it was I, who had been privileged to know her in what was the last month of her life. She fell asleep in Jesus on October 4th of that year.

God says, "Before you call I will answer," and never have I had this illustrated more clearly than in my experience of writing the book in your hands. Now that I knew the book was to be a priority, I struggled with the idea of how I was to get the time to write without interruption. As usual, God had things well in hand. I only had to be patient.

Shortly after this, my son sold some property to a businessman from out of state. This man was so impressed by my son's conduct that he called me to see if he and his wife could come up for a couple of days in order to get to know and observe our family. He wanted to see what we were doing that produced such outstanding young men. We agreed and enjoyed the time we spent with them.

Before they left, this man said, "Jim, I own a villa on the island of St. Croix. If your family ever needs a place to get away and just rest, it's yours to use for as long as you want, free of charge."

And here I had been wondering how I would get uninterrupted time. God had known and even worked things out so we could use our frequent flyer miles and spend a whole month of blessed peace and quiet on St. Croix.

I spent every morning in prayer, quiet contemplation, and writing. The afternoons were spent with my family on the beach, in the water, and under the water scuba diving. It was a relaxed and pleasant time that left my mind free to the impression of the

Lord's Spirit. I left that island with the skeleton of a book.

The chapters, the outlines, and the stories were mostly in place, but how to take that skeleton and create a manuscript was beyond me. I knew I needed an editor, but where could I find one? Several professional editors offered their services, but every time I prayed about it, the Lord always said, *No, this is not the one.*

I knew I needed more than someone to fix up my grammar, spelling, etc. I needed help with the writing, and if someone was going to write about my experience with the Lord, then I had to have someone who had the same experience and a writing style that blended with mine. Where on earth was I to find someone like that?

"Before you call I will answer." Again the promise was abundantly fulfilled. Several years prior, I had meet a couple named Tim and Julie Canuteson who wanted the experience I spoke on. As I counseled with them, we began to get to know each other and I saw them start making changes in their family, allowing God to work in their lives. Over the next few years, we exchanged letters and I was frequently struck by how similar Tim's conversational writing style was to my own. I would comment to Sally as I shared his letters that I often felt as if I was reading my own thoughts. He had an ability to take practical truth and put it into concise statements. I knew that they were starting to obtain the experience they had sought after.

Then in the fall of 1998, Julie walked into the lodge at our Virginia camp meeting and I sensed the Spirit's impression in my thoughts that here was the person I should ask for help. Julie loved English, and from previous visits I knew they had an interest in the editing process. I approached them, and they said they would be thrilled to look at what I had done.

I had no idea what I was in for. I sent off the first few chapters and they came back completely different. They had not just edited the book but had rewritten it and in the process took it from good, to better, and finally to the best. Soon we struck on the idea of my sending them just an outline with the illustrations I wanted to use along with a tape on which I would record my thoughts, my goals, and my aims for the chapter. In time, the mail would bring the finished product for my review. After a few chapters, I was delighted. I was thrilled to see God's hand at work.

This book was not to be the sole work of Jim Hohnberger but a joint project of people God had put in place and called to His service. I watched Tim and Julie as they worked to confirm their experience. They threw themselves enthusiastically into this project, never asking for any recognition, financial rewards, or even that their expenses be reimbursed. When I saw this humble attitude, I knew God had picked the right people. What I had expected to be a difficult task became a joy.

Today I stand amazed when I see what God has done. I must confess that, while human names may appear as the authors, all of us involved know that we did not write this book. It was God's book all along. As I encourage you to read it, I do so without a hint of self-promotion, for it was written through both the timing and the guidance of God, not by my hand or to my glory.

May all who read the words of this book grasp the purpose of its existence . . . to show the pathway of escaping to God.

CHAPTER 1

The Glorious Pursuit

"And it shall come to pass, that before they call, I will answer" (Isaiah 65:24, KJV).

"Jim, what are you doing way up here anyway?" Warren asked.

I could read his thoughts. Clearly he was convinced that I was wasting my life away up here in the mountains when I could be making big money down in the city. Warren had come up to look for wilderness property, and even now Warren, his pregnant wife, and I were bumping over back country roads in my truck to look at a property for them.

"Well, Warren," I began, "you see, I'm a Christian, and we came here because —"

"Stop right there, Jim!" Warren cut me off. "I'm not a Christian, and I don't believe in Christianity. I don't want to hear another word about it!"

The sudden cold hostility was unmistakable in the close confines of my vehicle. *How can God reach a person like this?* I thought. Nonetheless, I felt constrained to say something more and with a silent prayer I said, "Warren, all I need is a couple of minutes of your time and I will never say another word about Christianity. Warren, the God I've come to know in these mountains loves you so much that even though you are rejecting Him, some day when you need Him, He will be there for you. Some day you're going to need my God!"

If things were cold in my truck before, after these words they were downright frigid. It would seem I had made things even worse by my comments. We finished our business and Warren drove off, but the memory of our conversation reminded me of my own estrangement from God. The echo of my own words rang in my ears:

Some day when you need Him, He will be there for you. Some day you're going to need my God.

December 16, 1948

"Sir," said a tired looking doctor to get the attention of a man who appeared, if possible, to be more tired and worried than the physician.

"Yes?" Henry responded hopefully. His response seemed out of character in the worn waiting room with its lingering smell of tobacco smoke and the ever-present scent of fear and expectation, which haunts such rooms.

"It's a boy!" A ghost of a smile danced about the physician's sturdy face. "A 9-pound, 5 1/2-ounce baby boy!"

"Great! How's my wife?" Henry asked, already animated with the news of his son.

"It was a hard delivery." Concern was again evident in the expert's face. "You may see her now," he answered before the question was asked.

As I lay in mother's arms, I had no idea that at the moment of my conception I became a participant in the conflict between God and Satan. Even as I was formed in the womb, God, in His infinite wisdom, had set in motion an individualized plan to awaken in my heart a longing, a need for Him. He knew I was being born into a world that was at odds with Him, in rebellion to His principles, His will, and His ways.

God knew I was to be born with a nature damaged by man's

experimentation with sin. God also knew I would naturally follow my own impulses and inclinations and that the very thought of yielding my will and way to Him would be totally foreign. He knew all too well that Satan would oppose every effort He made. In spite of these odds, God set His plans for me in motion. After waiting almost six thousand years of human history for Jim Hohnberger to be born, He now had the opportunity to try and win my love. God was in pursuit of me as He is with every one of us. It is a glorious pursuit of love, born out of the heart of God.

Bernice and Henry Hohnberger were pleased with their third child. They took me home to their modest house in Appleton, Wisconsin determined to do all they could to see I grew up to be an honest worker and a good citizen. As an infant, I had no conception of a loving God and still God was speaking to me through my parents. They taught me my first lessons about the character of God by their interactions with me.

I was born with a self-will that wanted my way, now! When I was hungry—I cried. When I wanted my diaper changed—I cried. Whenever I didn't like something—I cried, in an attempt to get my way. When my mother met my needs she taught me, in a way she did not even fully understand, of a caring heavenly Father.

At times I cried because she put me in my crib and I wanted to be held. Mother had a choice—she could yield to my crying or she could teach me that I must yield my will and way to her. When she yielded and came to pick me up, she taught me that by crying I could have my own way, and the self-will growing in my little heart was strengthened. When mother said, through her actions, "No, you may not get me to pick you up when I have decided you need to be in your crib," she taught me how to yield my will to God's will by yielding to her will. Parents stand in the place of God to young children and by obeying their parents, they learn to obey God. Thus began the great tug-of-war in my life. Sometimes Satan would win a conflict and sometimes God won, but always I was growing and learning.

Growing inside each of us from birth is the desire to find fulfillment and happiness. Unless guided by wise parents and the grace of

God, this all too often means that we seek fulfillment in things. Things are not wrong, for when God made the earth, He filled it with things that bring pleasure, but the temptation is everlasting for people to place value upon the things rather than the One who is the giver of such things.

Think back over your own experiences of Christmases past. After tearing the gaily-colored ribbon and paper away to find some desired toy, we could scarcely express thanks to the one who had given us such a gift. Perhaps we mumbled a few words of thanks under our mother's prompting, but all our eyes could see was the treasured possession. The possession had taken the place of the giver.

For me, it was my new double-chrome plated, three-speed Schwinn bicycle. Oh, how I loved that bike! It was the finest in the neighborhood. Eventually, that love evolved into an affair with a fire engine red Pontiac convertible. I was slowly being trained by the world about me to equate happiness with the things I possessed.

Things consist not only of possessions, but positions, people, power, pride, and pleasure as well. Multitudes believe happiness and fulfillment come from attaining a prominent position invested with power and pride. Still others believe that being married to a certain person or visiting exotic locations will bring lasting joy. Others desire a life of pleasure seeking and freedom from responsibility hoping that this freedom will bring the true happiness.

All these things become a real source of competition for the affections of our heart, which are what God desires. God sees all this and His pursuit of us begins before we even have a desire to find fulfillment in Him: "Before they call, I will answer" (Isaiah 65:24, KJV).

Praise God that He plants within our hearts a desire for true fulfillment, which can but be dimly satisfied by the world's methods. There are evidences all around us of apparently successful people who have found wealth, power, and fame—everything that the world says should bring happiness. Yet, these are some of the most miserable people on earth, often ending their own lives in the wretchedness of drug-induced suicides.

In this controversy for human souls, the devil uses all the world's glitter and gold to seduce us. His methods use deception to make even our worst choices look good. He invades our minds and bombards our senses from every media outlet, magazine, and billboard. He appeals to our desires, passions, and appetites and seeks to enslave us. One need only view tobacco and alcohol advertisements to see how human beings become enslaved. The ads convey the idea that people who smoke or drink will become popular, sexy, and athletic. Instead, they soon find themselves slaves to a substance that robs them of their health, their money, and their happiness.

God is handicapped in this battle for our hearts. He never lies. He never misleads. He says, "Behold, I stand at the door, and knock: if any man hear my voice, and open the door, I will come in to him, and will sup with him, and he with me" (Revelation 3:20, KJV).

God appeals to our intellect, reason, and conscience. Our response has to be voluntary. He doesn't want robots. God can place a desire for Him within our hearts, but our response to that desire is entirely up to us. God never forces our will.

I didn't know I had a problem with self wanting its own way. It was all I had ever known. Still, God pursued and courted me for thirty years until I finally felt my need of Him. It took another ten years until He had gained my affections and then another six or so years until the citadel of my heart was fully surrendered and I was His.

The Bible tells of a man named Abraham who had been miraculously given a son in his old age. Like many a long-hoped-for child, this boy was doted upon by his father and quickly became the pride and joy of the old man's life. Abraham knew God—not just about Him. He was intimately acquainted with God.

Then God asked Abraham to sacrifice his son as an offering. "Take now thy son, thine only son Isaac, whom thou lovest, and get thee into the land of Moriah; and offer him there a burnt offering upon one of the mountains which I will tell thee of" (Genesis 22:2).

Why would God ask such a thing? Poor Abraham! How he must have suffered as he thought that his beloved son was being taken from him. With a heavy heart, he went forward to obey. God let the suffering old man go through with it right up to the point where he knew there would be no retreat, and then He stepped in and said in effect, "It's all right, Abraham. I never wanted your son as a sacrifice. Isaac, your son had usurped the place in your heart which only belongs to Me. I wanted to remove him from the throne of your heart so that I might reign there unchallenged."

Abraham was learning that God's gifts cannot become more important to us than the One who gave them. God does this with each of us. God pursues us until He has all of us. He didn't want Isaac as a sacrifice. He wanted Abraham. God does not want your things, but if those things have usurped the throne of your heart, they must be dethroned.

We often hesitate to give up our things to the Lord out of fear for their safety. This is especially true when those treasures are long cherished idols. But we need have no such fears. Jesus came not to destroy, but to save. Everything is safe when we commit it to Him and nothing is really safe if it is not so committed.

Six Months Later

I was traveling in the Midwest. While I was visiting with a family, the phone rang. The woman of the house said, "Jim, it's for you."

"Hi, Jim. It's me, Warren."

"Warren," I almost shouted, my mind traveling back to our conversation in the truck. "How did you ever find me out here?"

"It wasn't easy," he said. Suddenly the self-confident voice changed as he said, "We had that baby, Jim."

"Wonderful! What did you have?"

"I had a son . . . ." his voice trailed off.

"What's the matter, Warren?" I asked.

"Jim," he said, with anguish in his voice, "My son was born with three holes in his heart. I need your God, Jim! I need your God!"

Warren's anger and fear had been swept aside by his need. His story brought tears to my eyes as I was privileged to share with Warren the glad news of God's glorious pursuit for every human heart.

When I first asked my wife, Sally, out on a date, her potential responses were limited. She could accept or refuse. To be sure, to accept carried more risk. But to refuse would have been to forgo a lifetime of sharing the joy of a heart in tune with hers and a marriage made in heaven—what a sad alternative that would have been!

And so it is in this glorious pursuit of a loving God for the throne of our hearts. There are not a dozen possible responses—just one good choice and one very poor alternative. My choice has been to pick up that pursuit, which will not end till I stand face to face with the One I have come to know and love. What will your response be?

Religion—Is It Enough?

"This is life eternal, that they might know thee the only true God, and Jesus Christ, whom thou has sent" (John 17:3).

"But Mom, do I have to go? I don't like going to church. I never get anything out of it."

Of course, my Mother refused my plea, and I found my unwilling self attending church services every weekend. Church was such a burden to me that I must confess there were times I would sneak into the back of the church, grab a bulletin, and quickly leave for the park to while away the hour until I could arrive back at home with the "evidence" of my attendance.

It's not that my parents didn't try. They sent me to Christian schools and took me to church every week, but somehow church was just too artificial, too formal, too boring to reach me. I had to attend, so I learned at an early age to "play the game," so to speak. You probably know it yourself and not because you were a member of my church watching me. Many professed Christians go through the motions, doing what is expected—looking somewhat good on the outside but knowing their hearts are just not in it. They may not even be able to explain it, but it's just not meeting their true needs, and yet they follow suit because, well, it's the "right" thing to do.

When I was out from under my loving parents' influence, I quit attending. I pursued my interests and my way. Enough of this going to church and acting religious. When I added it all up, it amounted to no saving good anyway. God was no more real to me than He was to my non-Christian friends. Why continue the charade?

So I went my own way and God understood. He knew the churches I attended were promoting themselves rather than Him. He didn't blame me for walking away. He just waited for the right moment to get my attention.

I was thirty years old, had graduated from college and spent five years selling computer systems, and was now the sole proprietor of the Hohnberger Agency—a multi-line insurance agency, specializing in automobile, homeowner's, life, and health insurance.

I was young, aggressive, building a future, a retirement, and a comfortable present. I was "making it" in the world. I had a lovely home, new vehicles, a good income, and a prospering business. I was chasing the American dream, believing that happiness comes from the things that make life interesting, comfortable, and exciting.

Solomon, the wisest man who ever lived, summed it up so well when he said, "All is vanity" (Ecclesiastes 1:2). Vanity is emptiness, a mirage, something you can never get your hands on. I was pursuing this emptiness, this American myth, and God needed to get my attention. But how? He simply waited, and when the time was right He prompted me to sell life insurance to my dentist. Little did I know how drastically my life would be changed from following that one divine prompting.

My dentist was one of my clients. I insured his business, his home, his health, and his auto, so I couldn't see why I shouldn't sell him some life insurance too. I made an appointment to see him one day to do just that. He wasn't interested, which made no sense to me as I knew he was a reasonable man. "Why don't you want to purchase this life insurance plan?" I asked.

"Because I believe the Lord is going to return before I would need or benefit from such coverage," he responded.

I laughed at him! You hear all kinds of excuses in the insurance business, but this was ridiculous. I thought he must be joking. "What's the real reason?" I probed.

"That is the real reason."

"Where did you ever get that idea?"

"From the Bible. Don't you ever read the Bible, Jim?"

"The Bible! Why that's just a bunch of 'Our Father's' and 'Hail Mary's'!"

"Oh nooo, it's not."

So began an hour and a half discussion not on life insurance, but on life assurance. It really caught my attention. My interest was stirred and my curiosity aroused. He looked at his watch and said, "Jim, I have to get home. I have obligations. Why don't you and your wife come over Wednesday evening and we can continue our discussion then."

"I can ask you anything, and you won't be offended?"

"Of course," he assured me.

"Sounds great!" I said. "We'll be there!"

Wednesday evening, Paul and Ethel Conner greeted us warmly. After a few minutes of visiting in their living room, Paul suggested we move to the dinning room where the four of us sat around the large table. I contemplated how strange these people were. They hadn't offered us a beer or anything else to eat or drink and now as we sat at the table Paul excused himself to get something. I thought maybe he had belatedly remembered the beer, but no, he walked around the corner with four, count them, 1-2-3-4 Bibles! *Oh, no!* I thought. *He must be some kind of fanatic. Even the pope doesn't own four Bibles!*

Then Paul passed out the Bibles and said, "Jim, open your Bible to Daniel."

"What's Daniel?" I asked.

"That's a book in the Old Testament."

"What's the Old Testament?"

"You really weren't kidding when you said you didn't read the Bible," Paul said with a smile.

Sally and I left their house at 11:30 that night. We had never heard such startling truth in all our lives. These truths rang the bell in my heart that would eventually awaken the desire God had planted there for Him.

They invited us to come again the next week. I started to look forward to Wednesday night. Paul was a Bible scholar. He made the Bible come alive. "Why didn't anyone in my church ever tell me these things?" I demanded.

"I don't know," Paul said simply. "You would have to ask them."

That is just what I resolved to do. I knew two priests. I went hunting with one, and I went drinking with the other. So I asked one of them.

"Who have you been studying with?" he responded.

"Dr. Conner and his wife."

"No, Jim. I didn't mean the people you're studying with. I meant what religion are they?"

I told him. He said, "Why, they're fundamentalists, Jim."

"What's that?" I asked.

"Fundamentalists believe that when you read the Bible, you should take it literally. That is, you should try and do exactly what it says."

I was confused. "What's wrong with that? And what are we if we are not fundamentalists?"

"Jim, we are traditionalists. We believe that the Bible was written thousands of years ago and must be interpreted in light of the traditions of the church and today's society. That way, we don't have to live the same way they did back in those barbaric Bible times."

"Oh! OK, that makes sense."

Armed with this information, we continued our Bible studies with the Conners every Wednesday evening for the next eighteen months. I had no idea the Bible contained such truths. At the end of every study, Ethel would ask me, "Jim, how about coming to church this weekend?"

I would answer, "No, not until I am absolutely convinced that this is truth." This response had almost become a tradition for us, so her face registered shock one week when I announced, "This week I am going to church. I can't wait to meet the saints that are living this kind of truth!"

I was excited! This was going to be a big thrill, for if these truths had excited me, then surely meeting those who were living these truths would be a wonderful event. Paul and Ethel didn't seem quite as excited as I was. In fact, they looked a little uncomfortable.

"Jim," Ethel said, "There are a few things we need to tell you before you go to church . . . ."

Well, they tried to tell me what I would soon find out for myself. Not all the saints are saints. Later I would find the Bible speaks of this by saying, "For they are not all Israel, which are of Israel" (Romans 9:6), and "For he is not a Jew, which is one outwardly; . . . But he is a Jew, which is one inwardly" (Romans 2:28, 29).

Strong words, but little did I realize how soon they might be readily applied to me.

During those eighteen months, I began to have a love affair with God's Word. God was using His Word to awaken in my heart a response toward Him. However, I fell into one of the traps Satan lays for those seeking God. I felt that intellectual assent to the truth was all that constituted becoming a Christian. I truly believed, so much so that the truths contained in His Word became my religion.

I had longed all my life for someone to show me how to be a Christian and now I felt I had found the way. I had a strong will and as I discovered truths in God's Word, I would apply them to my life. I had zeal for my truths. I was sincere. I was honest. I was also dead wrong about what constitutes becoming a Christian.

My zeal led me to try and share with my family the wonderful "truths" I was discovering. As I tried to show them that their doctrinal positions were not biblical, they didn't like it. They would not accept my truths. Oh, they may not have been able to provide an explanation or defend their position biblically, but they refused to accept mine. This was baffling to me. For surely when they were convinced of the truth, they would want to obey it.

So I went back again and again, with even more zeal, until my family made it clear that not only did they not want to have anything to do with my new religion, but they really didn't care if they had anything to do with me either.

My attitude stated, "I'm right and you're wrong. I have the truth and you believe a lie." It totally turned them off, and rightly so.

Others noticed my zeal for outreach, and soon I was giving Bible studies to other earnest souls who, just like me, accepted the wonderful truths of the Bible as their religion. I became the head elder in the local church and looked good on the outside.

However, it became increasingly clear even to this stubborn German that something in this Christian life I was leading was not quite right. I could go to church and present a beautiful message about overcoming sin, and then I could go home, yell at my wife, and get irritated at my children. I knew this was not right, but even my strong human willpower couldn't seem to gain the victory in this area.

The Bible describes it like this, "Out of the same mouth proceedeth blessing and cursing. My brethren, these things ought not so to be. Doth a fountain send forth at the same place sweet water and bitter? . . . so can no fountain both yield salt water and fresh" (James 3:10-12). "If any man among you seem to be religious, and bridleth not his tongue, but deceiveth his own heart, this man's religion is vain" (James 1:26).

The Lord began to speak to me in such texts and a nagging suspicion started taking hold in my mind. Have I missed something? Am I really converted? I was in the church, but was I in Christ? I was in the Word, but was I in the Word that was made flesh and dwelt among us? It dawned on me that just because a mouse is in the cookie jar, it doesn't make him a cookie! Over a period of a couple of years the Lord finally got through my stubborn spirit and said, *Jim, you need to pull back and reassess what you're doing. You need to make sure you're converted.*

"Me? Why Lord, I'm the head elder of the church! I've brought more than a dozen people into Your church. Me, not converted?"

Yes, Jim, there are some things you just don't understand.

I came to understand that orthodoxy, or right doctrinal opinions, are but a slender part of true religion. Today, there are millions of professed Christians who hold "right" opinions, and yet has there ever been a time when true spirituality was at a lower ebb?

Sound biblical exposition is an absolute must for any Christian to survive the great events at the close of earth's history. Yet we may carry on the exposition in such a way that we lead the hearers into a system of "truths," rather than leading them to God.

For it is not mere words that revive the soul, but God Himself, and until the hearers find God in a personal experience, they are not always better for having heard "the truth." The Bible is not an end in itself, but a means, a tool to bring people to an intimate walk with their God. Christ speaks to us today with the same words He addressed to the outwardly religious scholars in His day. "Search the scriptures; for in them ye think ye have eternal life: and they are they which testify of me. And ye will not come to me, that ye might have life" (John 5:39, 40).

I had a theological understanding and could discuss my biblical exposition in learned terms, but if I could have come face to face with true living Christianity, my great knowledge would have appeared as foolishness.

If I could have stood at the foot of the cross and talked with Mary Magdelene, what would our conversation have been like?

"Mary, I see you didn't abandon Jesus like some of the others. Are you doing these good works through imputed or imparted righteousness? If you received righteousness from God, then you must have been justified. When were you justified? And was that forensic or intrinsic justification?"

"What? Who? Whatever are you talking about?" she might have asked. "I love Him! He's my Lord, my Savior! He redeemed me!"

Which one of us had true religion, the head elder or the harlot? I had all the theological terms, but she had the heart experience.

The organized religions may prove to be the greatest substitute for a saving knowledge of God that the world has ever known. A great danger lies in complacency. We have accepted the doctrines and attend weekly services, thus, we feel contented that we are safely in the fold. After all, we are in the church and in His Word, so we must have found God. But have we?

Church membership and profession have wrongly become synonymous with the new birth experience. Because everyone about us has approximately the same experience we possess, we see no danger and sense no need of a deeper experience. This situation exists in nearly all churches and denominations of our day and this spurious belief that we have found religion through knowledge, profession, and attendance alone allows us to treat God as a convenience rather than the nucleus of our everyday life.

The churches are for the most part dumbing down even the last vestiges of true religion that remains among them. They offer assurance and comfort apart from any true living connection with God. The members have become like a baby taught to be content with a pacifier rather than the "real thing."

It may sound as though I am against religion, but this is not so. While religion did not bring me to God, it was a springboard, a stimulus that has opened my eyes and started my thinking. It has been a catalyst, if you will, to point me in a direction, to ground me in some principles, and to provide me with some structure. Without this, few would ever enter the path to a deeper life. For this I will always be eternally grateful.

But I long for the people of these churches to see what has been forgotten; that God is a person and can be known and experienced by all. The intercourse between God and the soul is the heartbeat of the true Christian experience! Daily, hourly, moment by moment, God is directing, God is empowering, God is inspiring us to live a "life . . . hid with Christ in God" (Colossians 3:3) that "God may be all in all" (1 Corinthians 15:28). This is the experience I sensed was missing. I didn't understand it, but somehow I longed for it in my deepest soul.

God put that longing in my heart, and He wanted to give me this experience, but He knew it was going to require some major changes in my life. God knew I would never find Him amid the "churchianity" and "religiosity" of the world, with its pride, pompous pretense, and self-promotion. So He gave me the same message Jesus gave His disciples. He said, "Come ye yourselves apart . . . and rest a while" (Mark 6:31).

He was giving me the very first keys to this experience. First, I had to respond to His glorious pursuit of my heart and determine to find Him. "And ye shall seek me, and find me, when ye shall search for me with all your heart" (Jeremiah 29:13).

Then God said, *Jim, you must be willing to trim your schedule, reduce your never-ending commitments, simplify your life so you can "Be still, and know that I am God"* (Psalm 46:10).

CHAPTER 3

A Life of Simplicity

"In returning and rest shall ye be saved; in quietness and in confidence shall be your strength" (Isaiah 30:15).

Their convention was the largest the world had ever seen. From every corner of the earth came the delegates, worried because instead of destroying the competition, they themselves seemed in danger of destruction. This evening would be the keynote address by their extraordinary leader. The delegates talk to each other in hushed tones and repeatedly there is the hope that if anyone can turn the situation around, tonight's speaker can!

For as long as they can remember, he has been their leader. More than that, he is the one they all want to emulate. He has both their affections and their loyalty and over the years has become, in essence, their god. Thundering applause spontaneously erupts from the delegates as he appears before them and takes his rightful place at the podium. He looks out at the sea of eager upturned faces and like a politician, he feeds upon the crowd's approval. As the ovation calms, he takes a deep breath and begins.

"Listen, you devils! You aren't going to keep the Christians from going to their churches. They are going to go! You can't prevent them from holding their doctrines or from saying their prayers. They are going to do it! We must change our tactics if we are to enjoy continued success.

"Time is the key, my friends. We can concede them their doctrines, their prayers, and their churchgoing if we can control their time. Time is the essential ingredient, for without this they will never find a saving connection with 'Jesus'!" he said, spitefully spitting out the last word.

Satan went on. "Let them think they are saved, while we control their time and they are ours just as surely as those who never set foot inside a church. How are we going to do this? Simple. Keep them busy in the nonessentials of life and invent unnumbered schemes to occupy their minds. Encourage them to spend, spend, spend and then work, work, work to pay for it. Fill their mailboxes with catalogs full of the most enticing offers. Follow these up with credit card offers to pay for it all.

"Teach them that happiness comes from things and induce the husbands to work 8, 10, 12 hours a day, six to seven days a week. Make them work two jobs if necessary. Make it appear a necessity for the wives to work. Tell them there is just no other way, if they are going to maintain the lifestyle they want for their families. Then get the wives to work long, hard hours coupled with the home responsibilities so they have no energy left at the end of the day for their husbands or children.

"Overstimulate their minds so they cannot hear Jesus whispering to their consciences. Bombard their senses with music playing in every home, workplace, and store. Make sure that bad news hits them every day wherever they turn. Use newspapers, magazines, radio, and television, 24 hours a day.

"Corrupt the moral fabric of their marriages and their young people by placing sensual images that invite impure thoughts on billboards, in movies, newspapers or magazine covers, and, of course, on television. Use TV talk shows to parade the most deviant members of society through their living rooms. Have them hungrily feast upon the sordid details of immoral behavior until they begin to see evil as just another alternative.

"Have them dwell on the trash, trivia, and trouble of the world. Detail the misdeeds of the rich and famous. Distract them from serious realities of life by vain hopes with sweepstakes, lotteries, and gambling casinos. Fill their shelves with books, magazines, and still more books. These represent time; and more time spent here is less time spent with God.

"Fill their homes with computers and send them out on an electronic highway where we control most of the exits. Send them lots of email. Bog them down in the "spam" of never-ending information. Give them laptop computers so they can always be at work.

"Make sure everyone has a pager, even children. Fill their days with phone calls. Give them cordless and cellular phones so it is easy to talk all the time. Make sure their answering machine runs over with messages.

"Overwhelm the children with activities, sports programs in school and after school, dance, ballet, scouts, clubs, music lessons, proms, and parties. Stress them out with increasing amounts of homework at earlier and earlier ages. Send them to preschool and early childhood programs, get them away from the parents' influences and let them lead as separate a life from their parents as possible, so by the time they are teenagers, they have nothing in common with Mom and Dad. Have them so stressed that they will respond to our encouragement to be sexually active, to use cigarettes, alcohol, or other drugs as an escape.

"Even in their recreation let them be excessive. Send them on expensive vacations. Have them go, go, go! Have them return from their recreation exhausted, disquieted, and unprepared for the coming week. Don't let them go out into nature. Send them to amusement parks, sporting events, concerts, and movies instead. Make this saying your motto: 'Vacation makes them tired enough to go back to work and poor enough that they have to!'

"If they avoid these traps, use their own churches against them. Give them so many offices, responsibilities, and problems to deal with that their time is consumed in 'good works.' When they meet for spiritual fellowship, involve them in gossip and small talk so that they leave with troubled consciences and unsettled emotions. Bring crisis after crisis to their church so they are kept so busy 'putting out fires' that there is no time to kindle the flame of the gospel in their own hearts. Encourage them to study doctrines and evangelism. Let them attend training seminars, leadership workshops, and great church conferences on outreach.

"Clear the way for great interdenominational rallies seeking reformation. Be sure you get them to pay lip service to putting family first; to family values. Then get them involved with great social issues like abortion. Let them have conservative lifestyles but, at all costs, and in any way possible, keep them from coming to the Bible and to God as a sinner in need of salvation. For if they do, all is lost to us.

"Time is our greatest weapon and our greatest friend, my colleagues. Let us use it wisely and let them sleep in their deceptions just a little longer. Then both the world and the church will be ours and we will have won an everlasting victory. Go forth my friends to the victory!"

With both hands raised Satan exhorts his minions. "On to victory! On to victory! On to victory!" Until at last only the echo and results of this climactic meeting filter down to us today.

It was quite a convention! I may not have guessed all the details of the meeting, but you be the judge of the results. Evil angels went eagerly to their assignments causing Christians everywhere to get busy, busy, busy and to rush here and there. We are not living simple lives, my friends. Our lives are too congested. The whole system is overstimulated. Has the devil been successful at his scheme? The plan has worked beyond his wildest dreams.

Satan has managed to get the whole world aboard a fast-moving train. That train goes faster and faster and faster with each passing day, and he is unwilling to slow that train down so that anyone can get off. I spent more than thirty years of my life on that train, unaware of the path I was traveling.

You see, we humans are remarkably adept at not seeing the obvious. This insight was coming, but it would take a combination of one of the world's best known wilderness areas and a virtually unknown little lake to get us off that train.

Realizing that we needed some time away from the work-a-day world, Sally and I started planning what we called "time out." In late June of 1982, we packed the kids in the station wagon and headed up the northern peninsula of Michigan to camp by the shore of Imp Lake.

There was almost nobody around at that time of year and we set up camp and walked but a few feet from our camp to the lakeshore. Matthew, age 5, and Andrew, age 3, immediately started throwing stones into the water and while they were occupied, Sally and I sat on the beach and tried to relax. The rush was over.

I was on vacation for ten days of no problems, no phones, and no responsibilities outside of my family. Yet as I sat there on the beach, I felt as if my whole body was racing and I turned to Sally and said, "Honey, would you take my pulse?"

"Sure," she said, taking my wrist in her hand and reverting to her familiar role as a professional nurse. "It's 88."

"Is that good?" I asked.

"No, Jim," she said, her beautiful face clouded with concern. "That's not good for a man thirty-three years young who's just sitting on the beach."

A few days later, I was skipping stones on that same beach with my sons. They were admiring my efforts with an awe that only a young child has for his father's accomplishments. I felt relaxed, refreshed, and calm.

"Honey, would you take my pulse?" I asked again. The result was 68. I was astonished! The math was easy. Just by relaxing, my heart rate had slowed 20 beats per minute. That was a difference of almost 29,000 beats a day. It began to dawn on me just how much stress I was living under and what this stress was doing to my body.

This simple event set the tone for the rest of our ten-day vacation. What was life really about? For the first time I questioned success. If I made 100,000 dollars last year, do I have to make 150,000 dollars this year and a quarter million the year after that? Where does it stop, and when do I consider myself a success?

As I looked at my boys still throwing stones into the water, a shocking realization hit me and I painfully said to Sally, "I don't know my own sons." I knew who they were. I knew their names. I knew their pants size. I made sure they had food for their tummies, but I didn't really know them as individuals. What exactly was I chasing anyway? What was it costing us? We returned to civilization disquieted, full of doubts about the path we were traveling.

My successful marketing of insurance polices "rewarded" me with an all expense paid trip to Reno, Nevada. Everything that wicked city stood for was against what I had come to believe as a Christian, so I asked the company, "Can I have cash in place of the trip?"

"No."

"Can I have a trip someplace else?"

"No. It's the trip or nothing."

Sally and I looked at the map of Nevada and noticed that south of Reno was a place called Yosemite National Park. "Let's go ahead and take the airline reservations and that hotel room and let's go to Yosemite each day," I suggested.

Here was a chance for Sally and I to spend some time together and so it was agreed. We left Wisconsin for Reno and the MGM Grand Hotel in early August. Later, in Yosemite, we parked and walked up to a crystal clear stream rushing out of the mountains. It so captivated us that we sat beside it for an hour and a half just enjoying the song of the water on the rocks. The scent of the pines was so strong we felt as if we could take it right into our lungs with each breath. We climbed our first mountains with me wearing patent leather shoes of all things!

In that quiet setting beside those peaceful streams, climbing those majestic mountains, and in mountain valleys full of pinks and lilies, we heard God speaking to us in a way we had never heard Him speak to us before. After a number of days in this setting, His voice seemed incredibly loud and He was saying, *Jim and Sally, get off the train.*

We realized that to not decide was to decide. Every time God brings us a choice, we make a decision, even if the decision is to do nothing. God had said, "Escape for thy life; look not behind thee; . . . escape to the mountain" (Genesis 19:17).

Action was needed. We decided on the plane trip home that we were going to try to live the way we felt God was calling us to live. When God created man, He placed him in a garden prepared for him. We couldn't live in the Garden of Eden, but we felt that the closer we could come to God's original plan, the better it would be for our spiritual, mental, and physical health. We decided to follow God's call upon our hearts and like Abraham so many years before, we felt like pilgrims following our God to the Promised Land.

We were determined to put our plans into action. We put the house and the business up for sale. Then we pulled out a map of the United States and planned where we wanted to go. Right away some areas were ruled out. Neither of us like the hot, humid climate of the South. There were objections to some other areas. The search soon narrowed to three geographical areas: the upper peninsula of Michigan, northern Maine, and the Pacific Northwest. We had visited Glacier National Park a few years previously and felt drawn to this gem of the continent.

In September, we visited Montana again and extensively looked over the area surrounding the park. We were concerned that we might locate in an area that would build up around us, forcing us to move again. Finally on the western edge of the park, we traveled up one of the most beautiful wilderness valleys left in the lower forty-eight states. It was bordered on the east by Glacier National Park and on the west by the Whitefish mountain range.

We noted that 98 percent of the land was owned by the federal government. It was obvious that even if every piece of private land was developed, the valley could never be over developed. Glancing at each other, both of us raised our thumbs up. We had found our valley. We were going to Montana!

The valley runs sixty miles north and south with a beautiful wild river running down the middle. The population of our valley is 175 people in the entire sixty miles. There was only one forty-acre parcel of land for sale. The real estate agent informed us it had been on the market for five years! This was good news indeed because we had to sell our house before we could buy anything. If the property hadn't sold for five years, there was a very good probability it would still be there when we sold our house.

There were not many ways to make a living in this valley, but our plans did not include me working at first anyway. We wanted to use some of the equity from our house to allow me to stay home for the first few years to assist Sally with the boys and have time to develop a true connection with God. We were certain that the Lord had led us. We returned to Wisconsin with definite plans for relocation to Montana.

Our plans for relocation may have been taking shape, but our friends and families were adamantly opposed to what we were doing. The very idea struck them as fanatical, extreme, and foolish.

But we were determined to cut off every influence that hindered a full and complete surrender of ourselves to God. For our children, we would provide the very best environment possible. We would give them the best and guard them from all the rest.

Those who were most opposed were our fellow church members. "Your standard is too high!" they said. "It can't be done!" In a real sense, the world was more approving of what we were setting out to do than were our fellow Christians.

We were not survivalists. We only wanted to cut off the distractions that were preventing us from developing the relationship with God we longed for. We would eliminate from our lives those things that were good and, beyond that, even those things that were better so that we could possess that which was best!

Planning to purchase raw land had several consequences, the most important of which was that we had to sell our place by March if we were to get a house built and ready to occupy by the early mountain winter. Any later than this, and even with professional builders, we would be racing the weather. But March came and passed without a nibble on our home despite much advertising. I couldn't understand what was happening. I knew God had called us, and I felt He had led in our plans, and now I was bewildered. Friends and relatives started scoffing at us and tried to convince us that we had been mistaken. After all, the house hadn't sold by our deadline.

"Lord," I said, "did I misunderstand what You wanted?" At last, I withdrew the house from the market confused and discouraged.

In early May I got a call from a realtor who said, "I saw you had your house on the market a few weeks ago. I have a client who is interested in that type of property. May I bring him to see yours?"

"Certainly you may," I said. He brought a very interested client who spent a considerable period of time with us viewing the property and the equipment I used to maintain it. He wrote us an offer for six thousand dollars over our asking price, so he could purchase the tractor and mowers with the property. He paid full retail price for them even though they were now used. Hope sprang up anew. Again our plans were set in motion.

The next task was a rummage sale to reduce the excess of our lives, and we had lots of excess! Sally stayed to run the sale while I headed to Montana to buy our place!

Arriving at the Polebridge general store that has the only public phone for miles around, I called the real estate agent and found the property was still available. "I'm going up there to look at it one more time and then I'm coming down there to write you an offer for it," I said.

After examining the property again and feeling that it would indeed meet our needs, I returned to the general store and the phone at 2:30 in the afternoon.

"I'm sorry," the agent said, "but the property sold at 1:30 this afternoon."

It couldn't be true! In shock and disbelief, I called Sally with the news. Then disheartened, I went up a little hillside and prayed about the situation. *Jim, get into your car and drive up the valley,* the Lord said. Having nothing else to do, I turned northward toward Canada feeling very sorry for myself.

Towards the upper end of the valley I found myself pulling into someone's driveway, not even sure why I was doing it. An older man, obviously retired, was outside mowing what would have been grass, if there had been any grass. He was instead, mowing his weeds. *Well, I'll ask him about properties,* I thought. So I approached him and explained what I was looking for. He immediately said, "Well, I'll sell you my place."

"Is it for sale?" I asked.

"It is now," he replied.

He gave me a tour of the property and the little 960 square-foot log cabin. Slowly it dawned on me. God had a different place picked out for us all along. We bought that little log home on five acres overlooking Glacier National Park and bordering United States Forest Service land. Only later would we realize that the Lord had spared us a home building project. He was bringing us out to the mountains so we could build our characters rather than a house.

When I returned to Wisconsin, the pieces started falling into place. Sally had been busy. She made over ten thousand dollars at our rummage sale. The business sold. The details of the sale would, however, cause us considerable inconvenience in the near future. The purchaser was unable to replace me with another agent until some-time in October. The terms of the sale were that I would have to provide at least part-time oversight of the agency until the other agent was in place.

The house closed in early August and we moved our family to our Montana cabin. I barely had time to begin the settling-in process before I had to return and oversee the business. This left Sally and the boys to continue organizing in the smallest home we had ever owned. This was extremely hard on her, not only because she had to be both mother and father, but because we were both from a city environment. We had lived in the country, but our life there was little different than that of thousands of others residing in suburbia. Here she was, alone in the wilderness.

I worked like a dog at the agency so I could be caught up and return to Montana for another two weeks. There, I also worked frantically, not only getting settled, but trying to prepare for the coming winter and getting in a wood supply. So it continued back and forth, one week in Wisconsin, the next two in Montana, driving thirty hours nonstop each way until I was nearing exhaustion.

At last the new agent was in place and I made the final drive home to Montana. There was no one there! This was baffling, so I went down the road to the home of some people we had made friends with to see if they knew anything. Indeed they did! They were caring for my two sons. My wife, they informed me, had crashed from the stress and was in town at the doctor with pneumonia. It would take three months for her to fully recover.

At last we were together as a family in our wilderness log cabin. After paying off all our debts and paying cash for the cabin, we had a little bit of money left over—eighteen thousand dollars. We divided it into three parts and decided that we would live on six thousand dollars a year. We lived simply without things like paper towels and Kleenex. We couldn't afford such luxuries.

Then it happened to me. The stress I had been living under the last few months took its toll. I came down with pneumonia and was sick, very sick for a month. I was so weak I could hardly get up. Next, Sally broke her foot in three places, and there were corresponding medical expenses.

The water for the house was pumped out of the creek, but the weather became extraordinarily cold, and the creek froze all the way to the bottom. Now, we had two small children and no water except what we could melt from snow. Without water we had to use the outhouse rather than the septic system, and without the constant influx of water and organic waste to decompose, our septic system froze up too. Now we couldn't even put what little water we melted down the drain.

Our truck broke down. Sally fractured her foot a second time and then broke a finger on the neighbor's wringer washing machine. We filled the five-hundred-gallon propane tank used to fuel our generator only to have a bad valve blow out a week later.

We lost all our propane at a time we could least afford it.

Why was this happening? Was God still with us? We moved out to the mountains to find God and we had nothing but trouble and problems from the very beginning. Gradually it dawned on us that Satan was trying to discourage us and get us to move back to civilization where water doesn't freeze up, doctors are close by, and conveniences abound. We came to see that in all these troubles there was a message for us. If Satan was that concerned about us moving out here, then we must be on the right track.

The whole family took on the attitude that Satan would try to destroy us, but that if we were faithful, God would sustain us. Slowly that first winter passed. Finally, spring arrived and with it the restoration of our water supply. We had been hauling laundry to town so Sally was eager to wash some clothes at home. We didn't know the septic system was still frozen, and water poured all over the place. Hardships had become such a way of life that Sally and the boys were laughing as they moved bags of grain and other valuables out of the reach of the water and started to clean up.

It took time, but we became wilderness wise and learned to prevent water lines from freezing and to get in sufficient wood for the winter.

Our wilderness life didn't save us, my friends. It wasn't a magic cure. If you could have watched us in those first years you would have seen a family struggling to control itself. We developed a schedule and worked hard at fine-tuning it to meet the needs of our family unit. Sally and I set time aside for us and began to heal the marriage.

We finally had control over our time. With time to think and reflect came the opportunity to draw close to God. God was using wilderness living as a tool to draw us to Him without the distractions of the busy life we had led for all those years. Soon the tools that God had given us—a schedule, no distractions, the stern discipline of a simple life, and the grandeur of His creation—began to yield a result in our family.

We were drawn toward God and to each other. If you had known us before and could have visited us at this point, you would have seen the beginnings of the harvest of joy we were gathering from the hard choices we had made. You would have said, as we did, "It's worth it!"

Many see the need for drastic change, but how few are able to extricate themselves from circumstances. A minister's wife recently wrote to us: "When I called you, it was because prior to this I had come to the conviction that I needed to slow down, get on a schedule, and spend a lot more time in prayer and in the Word of God. I realized that my husband was not going to join me in my New Year's resolution. Nevertheless, I needed to be committed alone. I understood the concept of good, better, best. I truly wanted to choose the best.

"I have failed so miserably. I feel trapped right now. I have somehow scheduled myself as a Bible class teacher and leader, outreach ministries leader for two churches, fund-raising coordinator for two churches, health and temperance leader, community outreach helper, Vacation Bible School leader and teacher for two churches, newsletter and sometimes bulletin editor.

"Add to that the church work bees and the pastoral meetings I attend with my husband every single month. I also need to attend seminars for leaders, and about six other ministry related meetings every year with my husband plus board meetings I must attend because I have all these offices in the respective churches.

"As I am writing this, it seems crazy to have this kind of schedule in the light of the sanctification that needs to be done in my own life and keeping up with home duties in which my husband does not systematically cooperate. I am also in charge of the finances of our home, and I assist him as secretary many times. What do I quit? Where do I start? My life is a constant chase after unfinished tasks and upset people."

Who placed those burdens on the minister's wife? Certainly not God. She just picked up everyone else's expectations. A wise Christian wrote,

> "The Lord never compels hurried, complicated movements. Many gather to themselves burdens that the merciful Heavenly Father did not put on them. Duties He never designed them to perform chase one another wildly. God desires us to realize that we do not glorify His name when we take so many burdens that we are overtaxed, and, becoming heart-weary and brain-weary, chafe and fret and scold. We are to bear only the responsibilities that the Lord gives us, trusting in Him, and thus keeping our hearts pure and sweet and sympathetic" (*Messages to Young People,* 135).

Not that long ago, I was speaking at a series of meetings when a young woman gave me a note just as soon as I finished my sermon, which read, "Call Marie immediately!" Marie, a close family friend, and I hadn't talked in years. Oh, we would speak, but we hadn't talked, I mean really talked, in years. Why would Marie search for me in another state with a message like this, I wondered? Within five minutes, I was dialing her number. Her husband answered. "Praise God you called! Marie wants to talk to you!"

"What's up, John?"

"I can't tell you, Jim. I'll let Marie tell you."

Marie was in tears. "Jim, I'm so thankful you called. I just came from the doctor's office. He told me to make out my last will and testament. He says I'm a basket case. Can I come and stay with you a month? I need help!"

"Yes, come!"

"You're sure? Don't you want to pray about it? I thought you prayed about everything first."

"Marie, I have been praying about this for ten years. I don't have to get on my knees any longer. I've watched your life. I've seen what it's been doing to you. This is an answer to my prayers. I'll pick you up at the train station. Come!"

When Marie came, she had bleeding ulcers, pre-cancerous cells, and anemia, and she was as close to a complete physical and nervous breakdown as anyone I have ever seen. She was forty-six years old, and her hands couldn't stop shaking. Her eyes had that far-away look. I took her up to our little mountain home and settled her into our guest cabin.

What had happened to my friend? We were raised in the same town, on the same street. She got caught up in the American—I'm not going to say "dream," but—myth. She was working fourteen hours a day, six to seven days a week. She wanted to find that dream home. Then she felt she had to furnish it with exquisite furnishings. Life started controlling her. It was destroying her. It took her doctor to wake her up!

The modern American dream is a myth, but the myth doesn't only exist in America. It exists in Australia, New Zealand, Great Britain, all of Europe, Japan, Brazil, and all over the world. People are caught up in it, and it is destroying their lives.

I told Marie, "We aren't going to preach at you. We have a different lifestyle than you do. You can participate in anything you want to or feel free to reject anything you want to." Our whole family began to minister to her, and she became one with our family in our daily routine. She had worship with us in the morning and in the evening. She sang with us. She walked with us, ate our diet, played pick-up sticks and dominos with the boys in the evening, and joined in our family reading time.

My wife, a nurse, ministered to her in the health areas, and her health started to improve. As she slowed down, a desire for God was reborn in her heart. At the end of thirty days she told me, "You know, Jim, I can summarize my stay with your family in three words: less is more."

You see, we had a smaller home than she did. We had fewer

furnishings, less clothing, less in the garage, less of everything the world offers, but we had more of what the world can never give. We had love in our home. We had companionship. We had time for one another. That's why she said, "Less is more." I wish that commentary could be said of every Christian home.

I can almost hear someone saying, "The simple life is hard and dull, Jim." Hard perhaps, but dull? Right outside our back door we see elk and moose. The mountain lions and wolverines still roam free. The grizzly bear travels unhindered through these last primal forests. One day while hanging clothes on the line, I felt a strong nudge from behind as a huge buck put his nose in my back pocket looking for the little crackers we sometimes feed them. We had the blessed opportunity to tame a wild bear. She would allow us to pet her and would even climb on the swing set with my boys! Gaining the friendship of wild creatures is a little bit of heaven! Isn't that better than Disneyland? And when you get close to nature, you get close to nature's God.

My boys are never bored. All we have to do is say, Yes. Yes, you can go backpacking, canoeing, and cross-country skiing! Yes, you can go mountain climbing, rappelling, and track down that moose! Yes, you can explore those back woods! Yes, yes, yes! And yes, we will go with you.

Children in other environments are told no, no, no! Rebellion sets in. It is so much better to live where our children's choices are limited to choices between acceptable options.

By the way, simplicity is a stern discipline, but this is not a new sort of legalism. We do this with Christ so that we may bring Him into our marriage and families. It is not just some new reform that we all follow, thinking that we are the saved ones because we live the simplest life in the world. Christ lived a simple life and He is our example. The quiet simplicity of Christ's first thirty years prepared Him for the three and a half busy years of active ministry.

What is the Holy Spirit saying to you? Is He saying, "Get off the train"? God promises, "My people shall dwell in a peaceful habitation, and in sure dwellings, and in quiet resting places" (Isaiah 32:18).

We need to return and find our rest, to find that connection with God. When we experience that quietness and confidence, we will know that God is with us every moment and every second of the day. If we are going to find that living, vital connection with Jesus Christ, we must quiet our lives. We must simplify. "In returning and rest shall ye be saved; in quietness and in confidence shall be your strength" (Isaiah 30:15).

Not everyone is called to relocate to the wilderness but everyone is called to have the wilderness experience with God. You can start right where you are, simplifying your life and making time for God and family. It takes no special skills or significant sums of money to accomplish this, only a determination to possess this experience.

The text from Isaiah ends with the sad commentary, "and ye would not." Friends, it doesn't have to be said of you. Please don't let it be said of you! Today is the day, now is the hour. You can choose to escape to God and find rest.

CHAPTER 4

A Bundle
of Choices

"Choose you this day whom ye will serve"
(Joshua 24:15).

Our efforts at simplification had yielded wonderful results.
The busyness and distractions of life had been eradicated. But
this alone was not sufficient to bring me any lasting happiness or
peace. I knew the Lord had led us out to the wilderness for the
primary purpose of our spiritual development. While I had studied complex theological concepts for years, my studies had never
produced the type of character changes that I desired to have in
my life. I was still laboring under the misconception that more
knowledge, a more complete understanding, and a more perfectly
understood theology was all I needed to produce a transformation
in my life.

With this in mind I purchased five books from five well-known
and respected theologians. Here in the wilderness, I finally had both
the time and the inclination to obtain a working knowledge of salvation. Eagerly I started to read. By the time I finished the last
book, confusion, unlike any I had ever known, settled upon me. It
was clear that not one of the leading scholars agreed with the oth-

ers. If they couldn't understand or agree on the gospel, what hope did I have?

I knew in my heart of hearts that the gospel could not be as complicated as man had made it. Common sense told me that the true gospel would save me from those areas of my life in which my willpower had proved useless. That gospel would provide me with a power with which to control my feelings, my thoughts, and my passions. Through the guidance of the Lord I had made many changes in my life, and yet I still longed for peace with God. I still hoped for full assurance of salvation.

As I shared earlier, we realized early on that our suburban lives were too complicated, too busy. Only after we were in the wilderness did it begin to dawn on me that my theology was suffering from exactly the same problems that had so plagued our life in civilization. It was time, once again, to simplify.

I went back to the Bible with prayerful study. This time I didn't go to prove some theological position or to gain some doctrinal understanding. I went to the Word of God as a sinner in need of salvation. I knew that unless I found a better, a deeper, living experience capable of saving Jim Hohnberger from himself, I was lost! When I approached the Bible with that humble and teachable spirit, it became a living fountain. From its pages flowed a gospel message that was just as simple and had just as practical an application to my life as did the wilderness lifestyle that God had called us to live.

The Bible taught me a gospel message, which in its simplest form is about choices—simple, straightforward, everyday choices. Those choices, when combined together, compose the whole length and breadth of the Christian experience. It is my privilege in this chapter to share with you these choices, which have so transformed my life.

Some may complain I am oversimplifying the gospel. I truly do not believe this is possible. The gospel should be presented so simply that little children can understand it.

Others may accuse me of teaching salvation by works. Nothing could be further from the truth! Prior to discovering the true gospel, I spent my entire "Christian" life attempting to be good, to change myself, in my own human strength. Surely I understand the futility of such an experience. Yet, I am unashamed of the gospel of Christ, which not only can, but will, produce changes in the life of any man, woman, or child who accepts it. These changes are the inevitable fruit of the gospel.

Those who object to the fact that the Christian can truly obey and do good works have never tasted grace and experienced a power outside of themselves. This power "is able to keep you from falling, and to present you faultless before the presence of his glory with exceeding joy" (Jude 24).

So if you are inclined to be a critic, you may not look with favor upon the following pages. But if you, like me, long for something better than that which you have experienced, if you want full assurance of salvation, not just theological mumbo-jumbo, if you desire peace with God and the resulting peace within yourself, then turn these pages and explore with me this bundle of choices.

*   *   *

A newly married man and his wife started it all. As they sat in the departure lounge of the Salt Lake City Airport waiting for their flight, they visited quietly over the open Bible in his lap. The man was a recently ordained evangelical minister, and his earnestness and zeal were unmistakable. They were a hard couple not to notice, so obviously in love, and yet it was that open Bible which set them apart from the average traveler.

Al, a devout Mormon businessman noticed it too. He sat a little ways across from them as he waited for the same flight. He observed the pair as discreetly as possible, averting his eyes if they glanced in his direction. Al was a very proper man and would never want to be considered so rude as to stare at someone. Too late he realized that the young couple had been aware of his interest in them for some time. Suddenly the Bible shut as the young man stood and strode purposefully to this stranger whose attention they had so clearly captivated.

Al had visited my family a few short months before. He was a successful businessman in western Montana, not terribly far from where we live. He came to our home with two young Mormon missionaries. I assume the purpose of their visit was to enlighten me about Mormonism, but God appeared to have other plans.

Al became so enthralled as he learned of our lifestyle, our goals for country living, and our understanding of the gospel that he and I drew close together as we visited, forming the beginnings of a lasting friendship. Meanwhile the two missionaries were quiet and uncomfortable, hardly saying a word while Al undermined the very reason for their visit with his interest in our religion. I found Al to be a fascinating man, an independent thinker who was unafraid to examine his own beliefs and values. This rare trait endeared him to me and I was determined to keep in touch with him whenever possible.

Traveling near Al's office one day, I decided to visit him. He was genuinely glad to see me and after greetings had been exchanged, he proceeded to tell me of his experience at the airport.

"Excuse me, Sir," the young minister said as he approached Al. "I couldn't help noticing your glances in our direction. May I ask you a question?"

"Certainly," Al responded, while inwardly chiding himself for disturbing the quiet young couple.

"Sir, if our flight were to crash before we reached our destination and all of us were to die would you be sure of eternal salvation?"

"I think I would," my friend replied.

"That's not good enough," said the earnest young man. "You must know! Now let me ask you again. If you were to die today would you be saved?"

"I don't know," was Al's honest response.

"Listen," said the minister, as he flipped through the pages of his Bible. He read John 3:15, 16: " 'That whosoever believeth in him should not perish, but have eternal life. For God so loved the world, that he gave his only begotten Son, that whosoever believeth in him should not perish, but have everlasting life' " John 6:47:

" 'Verily, verily, I say unto you, He that believeth on me hath everlasting life.' " And finally John 11:25: " 'I am the resurrection, and the life: he that believeth in me, though he were dead, yet shall he live.' There," he said triumphantly. "Now, if you were to die today would you be saved?"

"Yes, I believe so," Al said.

"Then," said the young minister becoming animated, "you are a Christian and you have eternal life."

"You know," Al said to the young man. "I really admire your enthusiasm. I used to have that kind of zeal when I went out on my missions."

"Missions!" the young man squawked. "You used to go out on missions! Why, are you a Mormon?" he asked distastefully.

"Yes," Al said, bewildered at the sudden change.

"Why didn't you say you were a Mormon?"

"You never asked."

"Well, I'm sorry," said the minister, "but Mormons won't be in heaven." With those parting words he turned and walked away.

As he finished his story, Al slowly turned to me and said, "Jim, I'm confused. Can you shed some light on this subject?"

"I'll try," I responded. It was clear Al wasn't concerned about the unfair and prejudiced treatment he had received. He was intelligent enough to ignore the irrelevancy of the young man's bias. Al was struggling with the deeper issue of how to know, really know, whether he was saved or lost.

Lord, I prayed in my thoughts, *give me the wisdom and the words to satisfy this man. Help me to reach across the barriers we place between each other because of denominational affiliation and doctrinal bias.* As I turned to give Al my full attention I said, "Can I have a piece of paper so I can illustrate?" Al handed me a scrap of paper. I picked up my pen and began.

"Al, the Christian life is not made up of doctrines, creeds, reforms, or church membership. It is not even made up of beliefs, but rather the Christian life is a bundle of choices. When God brings a truth or light to our understanding, it always comes with a choice. We must choose to submit to the will of God or refuse. When God has all my known choices, then He has me.

"Let's say for purposes of illustration that the Christian life in its entirety is made up of a hundred choices," I said, placing the number on the paper. "Remember the thief on the cross?" I asked, looking at Al.

He nodded, so I continued. "Well, that thief didn't know a whole lot about the Christian life. His mind may have only been aware of a handful of the choices that compose the Christian life, let's say perhaps ten. But for those ten choices that he knew of, he was fully submitted to God. Christ could offer him full assurance of salvation not because of his great knowledge, but because he chose to surrender to God in <u>ALL</u> his known choices. Had he lived longer, he would have had the opportunity to advance in his Christian experience, and his choices would have deepened and broadened to encompass the whole gamut of the Christian life.

"Then there was Caiaphas, the Jewish high priest who wanted Jesus killed. He was aware of many truths in God's Word. He had lots of light, and that gave maybe seventy choices," I said as I scribbled down the numbers. "Yet, let's say that he made a free will choice to submit to God in only fifty of those choices. He had more choices, was surrendered in more of his choices than the thief, yet despite his greater knowledge and more choices, he was in rebellion to God. If he had been on the cross instead of the thief, Jesus couldn't have given him full assurance of salvation. Why? He had not submitted all his known choices and surrendered his will completely to God whereas the thief had."

"Al," I said, "do you believe that Jesus came to earth as your substitute and paid the price for your sins?"

"Yes, I do."

"Do you love the Lord with all of your heart and mind and soul?"

"Yes, I do."

"Then," I said, "you have accepted Jesus as your substitute. That is good, but it is not in and of itself complete. You must have Jesus as Lord of your life. Are you, at this moment, fully in submission to all your known choices? Are you at peace with God?

"No, I'm not," Al answered quietly.

"Then you have not accepted Christ as your Lord, and without accepting Him as Lord, your desire to have Him as your Savior is not sufficient to bring you either peace with God in this present life, or salvation in the life to come. For these two are inseparably one!

"You see, Al, the Christian life is not so much a matter of how much you know or how active you are, but whether all your known choices are surrendered in the present to the will of God. All the known choices of the thief on the cross were surrendered. Therefore, he was 100 percent God's, even though there may have been areas in his life that needed correction of which he was unaware.

"But Al, let a man, any man, stubbornly and persistently resist in even just one area, and this resistance will eventually lead him to join in the great revolt against God started by Satan himself. No matter how much we may desire Jesus to be our Savior, no matter how much we feel our hearts are drawn out in love towards Him, determined resistance to His leadership will in the end destroy us, just as it did Lucifer."

"I see, Jim. I've never understood this before," Al said, obviously struggling to come to terms with this new understanding. "Thank you."

My conversation with Al ended there, but there is more in that Bible story that we could understand. Two other men made choices we can learn from that same day. The first was Peter. He had followed Jesus for most of His active ministry. He had great opportunity and had been exposed to great light. Though just a simple fisherman, his exposure to Jesus may have given him as many known choices as the high priest. And Peter was in submission to most of them. However, in a few small areas, he would not submit. His desire for self-exaltation, his cultivated national pride, and his stubborn self-assurance were not surrendered to God. Thus he soon found himself denying that he even knew Jesus. He was

Christ's own disciple, and he failed because he had not submitted all his known choices.

Jesus is the other man who was faced with choices that day. Jesus demonstrated only surrender and submission to His Father's will in His choices, but the struggle is evident in His pleas to His Father in Gethsemane. "O my Father, if it be possible, let this cup pass from me: nevertheless not as I will, but as thou wilt. O my Father, if this cup may not pass away from me except I drink it, thy will be done" (Matthew 26:39, 42).

He had to choose just like we do. If we will adopt Jesus' attitude of "not my will but Thine be done," it will lead us to choose correctly even when we don't feel like it.

It is at this point that many are confused and finding difficulties in living the Christian life, for becoming a Christian is not a one-time choice but rather a minute-by-minute, continuous choice to let God have all of me.

Day in and day out I am to live for Jesus. My focus is to be in His will, His way. Many attempt to accomplish this through their own humanity. They set out with their strong willpower and their teeth gritted in determination to live the Christian life. It always ends in defeat.

How then is it possible to live every day, every hour, every moment to the glory of God? It's very simple. We are to live as Jesus did. Every morning Jesus took time with God. We too, must take time to give ourselves to God every morning, to surrender at the beginning of every day. It can't be a rushed thing but has to allow time for us to commune with God and really listen to what He's saying to us individually. God speaks to us through the Bible, nature, providence, and the impressions in the mind. Then after communing with our Father and making sure there is nothing to prevent us from hearing His voice, we can rest assured that He will guide us.

When we leave our place of quiet devotion, it is essential to take God with us in order to commune with Him throughout the day. We need to learn to ask, "What wilt thou have me to do?" (Acts

9:6). God wants us to know we are not in this alone. We need help from a source outside of ourselves at the beginning of the day and then all through the day. As we learn to be sensitive to the Holy Spirit's promptings upon our hearts, and learn to submit our wills to always do His will, then it is that ". . . Christ liveth in me" (Galatians 2:20).

But then temptation comes, perhaps the very same temptation that we have often yielded to before. In the past, we have gritted our teeth and tried to resist the temptation until we either failed or forced ourselves to obey. There is no peace or joy in such an experience. Friends, the true conflict of temptation occurs in the heart. I first must decide if I want to remain surrendered to God. When surrender is my choice, then self dies, the victory is won, and God supplies all the power to meet the temptation.

This experience is hard because self must die, but it is the only path to peace and joy as a Christian!

Now, choice doesn't merit me anything with God. I am not saved by my choices. The very desire to make the choice of submission to God is a gift from His grace. Salvation is fully the gift of God, yet it is that choice to submit that allows God the freedom to transform our lives through the ministry of His grace upon the human heart.

It is vitally important to see this, for most who have taken the name of Christ live a strange amalgamation of Christ and self, contending for the management of the life. This type of Christian life is like a yo-yo, continuously up and down. Being born of the Spirit is going from this experience to allowing Christ to be sole ruler of the life. When this amalgamation ends, there is rest for the soul. Then we learn the true science of salvation and the language of heaven, which is simply how to allow Christ full access to all my decisions and then by His grace, through a living faith, to say Yes to God and No to self.

Every choice to which we are brought offers an opportunity for us to choose to surrender our will and way to God. The Bible speaks of this as a death to self. Christ illustrated it this way, "Except a corn of wheat fall into the ground and die, it abideth alone: but if it die, it bringeth forth much fruit" (John 12:24).

How is wheat grown? It must be buried in the grave, so to speak, and for the rest of the plant's life it draws its strength from this grave. Christians must live in the same manner, rooted in Calvary—not merely an assent to Calvary, but a true entering into a Calvary experience.

No, we cannot die for sin as Christ did, but we can die to sin. Paul wrote about this in Galatians 2:20: "I am crucified with Christ: nevertheless I live; yet not I, but Christ liveth in me: and the life which I now live in the flesh I live by the faith of the Son of God."

Paul also said, "I die daily" (1 Corinthians 15:31). Obviously Paul did not literally die daily but what he referred to is the true Christian experience where we must die to self daily. We are encouraged to "reckon . . . [ourselves] . . . dead indeed unto sin, [and self] but alive unto God through Jesus Christ our Lord" (Romans 6:11).

The choice of putting self to death and submitting to God's will is well-illustrated in Scripture. Perhaps 2 Corinthians 4:11 says it best: "For we which live are always delivered unto death for Jesus' sake, that the life also of Jesus might be made manifest in our mortal flesh." This is true Christianity. Let me illustrate.

One cold winter morning not that very long ago, I awoke at my normal time and spent more than two hours in Bible study and prayer. I seek after God in the morning, knowing my own weakness and realizing that yesterday's experience will not save me from today's trials. Every morning just before breakfast time, we gather together to worship God as a family and to ask His guidance and protection throughout the day. It is a special time for our family that draws us together in strong bonds of love, which lasts throughout the day.

After our family worship time, I looked out the window on the beautiful sight of sixteen new inches of white fluffy snow. My wife was making waffles, and I could see the blueberry sauce bubbling on the stove to go over them. Now, I love waffles, and adding the blueberry sauce is just like icing on the cake. With one of my favorite breakfast meals underway, I decided to take a few minutes while the waffles were cooking and plow out the driveway.

We get a lot of snow in the mountain valley where I live; many, many feet of it each winter, and there are several ways we can remove that snow. I can use a snow shovel—the hard way—or I can use our large snow blower—better—but shortly after moving to the wilderness, I decided I needed a plow to fit on my Toyota Land Cruiser.

You will remember that we were living on a very small income and a three thousand dollar western plow with hydraulic lift was totally out of the budget. However, using a little ingenuity and investing about sixty dollars in some lumber, I built a V-shaped plow out of beams of wood and covered it with tin. I attached this to the front of my bumper, and it would free float over the road, clearing the snow and saving me huge amounts of time.

I was very pleased with my homemade plow, and while it wasn't necessarily beautiful, the effort it saved me was beautiful. Traveling down my driveway with the snow flowing off the plow to each side, I was enjoying the Christmas card scenery and having a great day with the Lord. My driveway is a third of a mile long, and towards the end I could see that there was a great big berm of snow left by the huge county snowplow.

I sensed the still, small voice of God warning me that I should not try and fight my way through, but I reasoned it away. After all, I had plowed through piles of snow before. The plow rode up over the berm then dropped down toward the road surface. In the meantime, while the plow was dropping downward, my vehicle was driving up over that big pile of snow. So, when the front end of the vehicle started to drop back down toward the road, it lodged firmly on top of the plow, holding it in the air. The front tires were useless.

My four-wheel-drive vehicle was stranded. I was stuck with my truck blocking the road, and I began to get concerned because where I live there is a long, blind curve, and anybody coming up that way could easily hit me without ever having a chance to stop. Just as this anxiety began to rise in my flesh, the Lord called for my heart.

Jim, surrender it to Me, that still, small voice said.

I had chosen that morning to surrender all my choices to Him. Now I had to renew that choice, and even though I hate inconveniences, I chose to surrender my thoughts and feelings. Then I quickly added, "Lord, I am in a dangerous position here. I know our road gets very little traffic, but please don't let me get hit out here."

There was only one thing to do. I was going to have to get under the vehicle and jack up the front end. This would enable me to disconnect the plow and pull it out of the way. With the plow out of the way, I could lower the vehicle to the ground and reattach the plow.

Crawling under the front end I found myself immediately facing a new frustration and temptation to let go of Jesus and give vent to my feelings. You see, when you are plowing fluffy white snow and you crawl under a hot engine, all the snow that has been kicked up on the undercarriage melts. I felt like I was in a shower. It was dripping down my exposed face and neck. As if this wasn't bad enough, the drops fell in my eyes, which would have been irritating with clean snow melt, but this melt carried with it all the grime of the undercarriage right into my eyes. Immediately, I wanted to feel sorry for myself. I was so tempted to say poor me and have a pity party.

Yield it to Me, God called, in His quiet voice to my thoughts.

"But Lord," I responded. "I don't like this!"

Jim, it is not a question of whether you like this. It is a question of your willingness to surrender even these irritations to Me. You see, self-surrender is the substance of the teachings of Christ. I was still learning this hard lesson.

"OK, Lord, You can have these circumstances," I responded. "Just don't let me get hit here in the middle of the road."

Almost instantly, I could hear another vehicle coming down the road. *Oh, no!* I thought, and as I rushed to extricate myself from under the truck, I struck my head on the back of the engine. It was a nice hard whack, the kind that raises a lump on your skull. "Lord," I said, "this just isn't fair, and I don't like it!"

Surrender those feelings to Me, Jim. Don't yield to them. I'm with you.

Once again I had to choose, and once again through the grace of God I submitted to God and gained the victory over my thoughts and feelings. Faith is not only belief in God but also a surrender of all my choices to Him—daily, hourly, moment by moment.

Looking over at the vehicle on the road, I noticed it had stopped, and two men got out. They were trappers and came over to investigate. They looked at my plow and the mess I was in with amusement. They hadn't even said Hello to me, and they were making fun of my plow. I wanted to straighten them out, but the Lord spoke to me again and asked me to surrender the irritation to Him.

"Why don't you get a real plow?" one of the men said.

I could just feel the anger rising in me. My flesh wanted to rise up and fight back, and again Jesus called to me to surrender it, and by His grace through faith, I made the choice to surrender those feelings to Him. The gospel is quite simple. It's just a matter of saying Yes to God and No to self. That's a faith that works.

"Look," I said, "I'm in quite a fix here. Do you fellows think you could hook up a chain to the front of the plow and use your truck to pull it out from under me? That way I can hook it back up in just a minute and get out of the middle of the road, so you guys can continue on your way."

They consented to do this, and within minutes I was back in business. I thanked them, and they went on their way. My youngest son Andrew came down the driveway at this point. My wife knew how long it should take to plow the drive, so she figured there must be a problem and sent him down to check on me.

Seeing that I was OK he asked, "What happened?"

"It's a long story," I told him.

"Well, as long as you're all right." Andrew continued, "I am going to go down to the neighbors'. They're away, and I promised to feed Odie for them."

I felt as though I had just fought a war and had won. It was only nine o'clock in the morning, and I was exhausted. In the past any single one of those inconveniences would have been enough to make me let go of Jesus and give way to self. Sadly I could recall, all too well, that when I would let go and give in to the frustrations, I would take it out on my wife and family. I would be grumpy with them as if it were their fault. You see, that's what sin does in our lives. It makes us, and everyone around us, unhappy.

"Andrew," I said "why don't you hop in, and I'll drive you down there. You can feed the dog, and I will plow out their drive. That way, when they get home, they will be pleased that they don't have to dig themselves out."

"Great!" said Andrew and down the road we went to the neighbors'. Turning down their long, sloping drive, I had plowed most of the way to the house when I came upon four trees that had fallen over the driveway in the snow.

I was stuck! I couldn't back up their drive because of the homemade plow, and now I couldn't continue forward. I felt like I should never have gotten out of bed that morning. Again I had to choose to submit my feelings and thoughts to God. For it is only by a constant renunciation of self and a continuous dependence on Christ that we can live the Christian life.

"Andrew," I said at last, "go ahead on in and feed their dog, and I will get on the radio and ask Mother to send Matthew down here with the chain saw so we can remove these trees and be on our way home." So, off he went to the house. Sally promised to send Matthew right down, and I got out of the truck to look the situation over, only to glance down and see that I had a flat tire.

"No, Lord. This is just too much. I don't want to have a flat tire!" I wailed. Right then and there, I heard Satan's mocking suggestion. "Give it up! It isn't worth it." Then just as quickly, I heard God's encouraging voice:

You don't have to let go, Jim. You can choose to hold on if you want to.

"All right, Lord. I will submit this to You. But I'm getting tired, Lord." I got out the jack and proceeded to change the tire, by which time Andrew was back.

"Odie won't let me in the door!" he exclaimed.

I wanted to get upset at yet *another* person, and again I felt the constraint of the Lord to keep quiet and speak gently to my son. Matthew should have been here by now, but he was nowhere in sight, and once more the flesh wanted to rise and think all manner of evil about my son because he was not there by the time I felt he should be.

Jim, God's still, small voice spoke in the quiet of my mind, *yield those thoughts to Me. You have held on this far. Don't give up now. I will never leave you nor forsake you. Please don't forsake Me, Jim.*

"OK, Lord. I'll just go and look for him."

Starting out to see what had become of Matthew, we had barely climbed up the drive before he came panting down hauling the chain saw. What struck me most was that he had obviously been working hard. He was perspiring and just covered in sawdust and wood chips from the chain saw.

"Father, I have been cutting down the trees leaning over our driveway and—"

"Never mind, Son." I said. "We'll talk about it later." There was no way I could trust myself to speak to my son. The promptings of the Lord were clear. Besides, it mattered not where the communication had broken down, the chain saw was here now, and I could almost taste the waffles.

"Matthew," I said, "you get in and drive the truck, and I will go in front of you and saw those trees out of the way." This is what we did, and shortly the last tree was removed.

I told the boys, "Listen, I'm going to clear the area by their garage. Matthew, you go down to the house with your brother and help him feed that dog. Odie knows you really well. I'm sure he'll let you in."

As I finished the last couple of swipes in front of the garage, I could see the boys were having problems. The dog was not letting them on the porch to feed him.

"He's not letting us in," Matthew said.

The temptation to complain about my boys immediately rose up in my flesh and I wanted to say, "Can't you guys do anything by yourselves!" Thankfully, the Lord had not left me. He was still there, pleading for my heart. The devil was saying, *Let go! Go ahead and let go!* God was there too. He was whispering to me. *Hang on Jim! Hang on to Me. You don't have to let go of Me and say words you'll regret.* None of us have to let go. It's always a matter of choice.

"Listen, boys," I said. "I'm going to grab hold of that dog, and when I do, you run in there and put that food and water down as fast as you can. Then we will go home and have breakfast. I'm hungry!" Then to myself I added, "Lord, please don't let that dog bite me! That would just be too much!"

Odie is not a little toy poodle. He is an Alaskan Elk Hound and just as big and tough as the name of his breed. I grabbed the dog and got him in a headlock. He was growling and snuffing and fighting for all he was worth. My boys never moved so fast as they fed and watered that dog. They were out of the house in short order. As soon as I let go, he ran over to his bowl and started to eat. I shut the cabin door and climbed wearily into the driver's seat.

"You're doing great, Father!" my boys encouraged me. No one knows us, or the struggles we go through, like our families. My boys knew that their father would normally have been in real trouble with only a fraction of the problems we had faced this morning.

"Well, praise the Lord," I managed to say weakly. "But I'm getting tired. I feel like I fought World War I, World War II, and the Vietnam War all by myself this morning. Thank God it's over, all over," I said, pulling into our driveway.

Amos 5:19 tells of a man who had lots of trouble. He was fleeing from a lion when he ran into a bear. Escaping both, he finally he got into a house and leaned his hand on the wall only to have a serpent bite him. That's the kind of morning I was having. I had been running from the lion and had evaded the bear and guess who was waiting for me at home?

That's right—the serpent. There never is a time when the Christian can relax and say it's all over. That's just when the devil loves to kick us, knowing we are tired and starting to relax. The words "Thank

God it's all over" were hardly out of my mouth, when the bottom of my plow fell off, stopping me almost within sight of the house. "Lord," I breathed to myself, "this is not fair! I'm very tired. I can almost smell the waffles, and now another problem."

You're right, Jim. It's not fair the trials you are having this morning, and it was not fair that I should have to leave heaven to die for your sins. Jim, fairness has nothing to do with the situation. You have a choice! This may be unfair, but you can still surrender it to Me and gain the victory.

"Very well, Lord," I said, "You can have it." I went to the garage to get a hammer and some nails. Andrew got out the snow blower to clean the area around the garage, and Matthew went in to help his mother. I continued to wrestle with the plow. I had placed a false bottom on the plow to keep snow from accumulating inside it and weighing it down. Now I nailed it back in place and pulled up to the house.

As I approached the garage I could see Andrew pushing our snow blower around the corner of the garage. You don't push a snow blower! They are self-propelled. This could only mean one thing. It was broken! NO! I just couldn't take another problem. I felt tired and weak. My blood sugar was down. I was shaky, and as I walked toward Andrew, I could hear God calling to my heart, calling for me to surrender. Instead, I chose to vent! I gave way to irritation. I blurted out in harshness and anger, **"WHO DID IT?!"**

Andrew just stopped dead in his tracks and said nothing. Matthew and Sally had come out to the porch to call us in to eat, and there I was. Everyone had seen and heard what had happened. I lifted up the snow blower and dropped down on my knees to look for the problem. I could hear God calling on my heart. *Come back, Jim. Make things right!*

But I wasn't sure I wanted to. Looking at the snow blower, I could see that a little set-screw that held the gears in contact with the drive shaft was missing. We live in the wilderness, and it is a three-hour round trip to town to get a new set-screw. Closing my eyes, I said, "Lord, if there is any mercy, please be merciful to me and forgive me."

Opening my eyes, I saw something out of the corner of my eye—a little black speck. Walking over to where it lay, I saw it was the set-screw. The Lord had allowed me to see more than twelve feet away in sixteen inches of fresh snow. What a good God we serve! I replaced the set-screw and joined my family at the table for our belated breakfast.

I had a grin on my face that went almost ear-to-ear. My family was incredulous! I could easily read their thoughts. *How can you be smiling? You just let go. We all saw you do it!*

"Look," I said to my family, "I know you are wondering why I am so happy, but today I held onto Jesus in more trying circumstances than I have ever held on to Him before. I gained victories over irritation today that I have never gained before. Yes, I know that I failed out there with the snow blower, and yet I didn't wait for an hour or a day or even several days to return to the Lord. I repented right away and asked His forgiveness, and now I ask yours. I'm excited not because I failed, but because I can see the Lord working in my life and I know that He who has begun a good work in me will finish it!"

Praise God, externals don't need to control us. When we learn to choose Christ as first, last, and best in everything continually, soon our choices become habits, and habits form our character.

For example, my family was privileged to spend a month on the island of St. Croix. This island, a former Dutch possession, retains several European customs. The one we noticed most was driving on the left or the wrong side of the road as we view it. After obtaining a rental car from the airport, I pulled over and told the whole family that they were going to help me drive this car because absolutely everything was on the wrong side. It was the most awkward experience I can recall. I had to force myself not to revert to old driving habits.

Amazingly enough, after thirty days I found that I could drive about without even thinking about overcoming the old habits. I had retrained myself, and now it was as easy to drive this new way as it had been the old. On our return to the United States, we wondered whether we would have the same kind of adjustment back to the old ways. There was no transition at all. We could still drive just the same as we always had.

Here is a lesson we could readily apply to the Christian walk. It is hard for us to change the manner in which we have always responded to God, and many who start to walk with God find it so awkward and so crucifying to their self-will that they are inclined to quit. Yet if they persevere, they will find it becomes easier and easier to submit.

However, just as we found we could still drive in the U.S., so will the Christian find that he can still choose at any time to go back to the old life of sin. Choice is precious to God, and He never takes the power to choose away from any of His children. He has instead given us a bundle of choices. Those choices determine our eternal destiny as well as our present happiness. Escaping to God is simply returning all our choices to Him continually until habit becomes character and we are fully His!

CHAPTER 5

Where You Are — God Is

"Surely the Lord is in this place; and I knew
it not" (Genesis 28:16).
"Lo, I am with you alway, even unto the end
of the world" (Matthew 28:20).

It seems that this is exactly where we ended up—Polebridge, Montana, the end of the world. Fifty miles separate me from the nearest paved road or electric utilities. But a few short miles to the north is the Canadian border. Due to the relatively scarce population of our wilderness valley, an accident or injury can be a serious, life-threatening situation. There may not be anyone passing by for a long time, perhaps hours, maybe days. Thus, our reliance is ever upon our Divine Companion. He never leaves us alone!

Fall in the mountains is a beautiful season of crisp days and fantastic colors. This particular fall day would find my wife home schooling the boys while I headed out to cut some firewood. Experience had been a good teacher. I was determined not only to obtain sufficient firewood for the coming winter, but to work toward my long range goal of always maintaining two years worth of wood on hand. I wanted to be prepared in the event that I was injured or sick and couldn't do hard physical labor. A two-year supply would give me sufficient reserves to avert a crisis.

Up the valley at Teepee Lake, I pulled off the road in an area where I had noticed some standing dead wood earlier in the season. As I parked my vehicle I saw up on a little ridge, not more than thirty feet high, that a tree had fallen and was wedged between two other trees. It was about eighteen inches in diameter, gray, clearly dead and dry, so I made a mental note to save room for that tree and proceeded to cut the other trees I had come for.

Climbing up the little ridge, I stood on the downhill side of the tree and started working from the top of the tree toward its base, cutting 16-inch sections of log for my wood stove. As each section of log fell to the ground, I would take my heel and gently push it off the edge of the ridge behind me to roll down the steep incline. The logs came to rest near my vehicle.

This was a great system and, while it required me to stand at the edge of the drop off, there was sufficient room to complete the operation, so I never gave the process a second thought. As I reached the section that was wedged between the trees and began to make the cut that would free the trunk, I sensed the impression in my thoughts that I should move to the other side of the tree. I reasoned it away. After all, my system of cutting off the sections had worked perfectly.

However, that morning I had asked the Lord to guide and direct me. I desired Him to be my constant Companion and had told the Lord that when He impressed me to do something, I would obey. The impression came again and this time I paused. "Lord, is that You? Are You asking me to move to the other side?" I silently prayed.

Yes, Jim, came the distinct reply.

"OK, Lord," I said, changing my position to the other side of the tree, "but this is ridiculous."

Completing the cut I had started on the other side, I stared in astonishment as several hundred pounds of log snapped outward toward the very spot in which I had been standing moments before. I hadn't realized that when the tree had fallen, it had wedged in between the other trees with tremendous tension. It had been, in essence, spring loaded, just waiting for me to free it with that last fatal cut.

I felt weak as I realized what that impact would have felt like had I not moved. That log would have transferred the kinetic energy of its movement into a crushing impact with my legs about the level of my knees, catapulting me off the edge of that ridge with the chain saw still running in my hands to land some thirty feet below. I probably would have been killed outright by the impact and subsequent fall with the saw. If not, there was little chance I could have survived until someone found me. No one knew exactly where I was.

I understood without a doubt that the Lord had saved me from, at the very least, serious injury and, more likely, death. I was learning that the Lord was there, even in that wilderness valley, ready to help me before I ever realized that help was needed.

Ephesians chapter 2 verse 8 says it this way, "For by grace are ye saved through faith; and that not of yourselves: it is the gift of God." Grace is God's continual presence in my life. It woos me, entreats me, and beckons to me, trying to save me from myself. If I will but listen, the Spirit will guide me, empower me, and protect me.

If God does all of that, then what is my part? I must be willing to continually surrender to the Spirit's moving. That's faith! It's a conscious choice to cooperate with His presence. It makes all the difference between being catapulted off the edge of a steep ridge and staying in step with our Divine Helper.

Glacier National Park and the surrounding area holds the largest concentration of grizzly bears found in the lower forty-eight states. Every year brings us stories of bear attacks on the human visitors in the park. Now, bears do not read survey maps. If they did, they would notice that in crossing the river they leave Glacier National Park and enter the U.S. Forest Service land, which borders our property. But man-made boundaries mean nothing to these creatures, whose actions are unpredictable at times.

When we moved to the mountains and took up residence next

door to these grand animals, we had friends seriously suggest we arm ourselves against the threat posed by these wild creatures. I rejected this idea. I couldn't believe that the very same God who had led us this far was going to allow us to be attacked and eaten by a bear. Hence, I rested in the knowledge that the Lord would be with me, for it was God's grace that had brought Sally and me to this pristine wilderness valley.

Sally's adjustment to our furry neighbors was hindered by her past experiences. When she was young, her older brothers had teased her by telling her that a bear lived under her bed and was going to jump out and get her. Until old enough to realize the foolishness of such a concept, she lived in fear that this would really happen. So my dear wife came to the wilderness of Montana with a long-standing and deeply-cultivated fear of bears.

The problem was that in Montana the bears were no mere objects of childhood fantasy; they were a grim reality as far as Sally was concerned. While these real bears might not jump out at her from under her bed as she had grown up fearing, they could and did step out of the woods without the slightest warning of their presence. Only those who have had contact with wild bears can appreciate how quietly such a large animal can move through the woodlands.

It is a hard thing to put away cultivated fears, even harder if those fears have some basis in reality. That's just what Sally had to do and it was a struggle. She had read that ". . . perfect love casteth out fear" (1 John 4:18). She also read, "And I the Lord will be their God . . . and I will make with them a covenant of peace, and will cause the evil beasts to cease out of the land: and they shall dwell safely in the wilderness, and sleep in the woods" (Ezekiel 34:24, 25). Time and again, these old fears would rise up as real as ever, and her only escape was to surrender them to God and trust in her faithful Companion. Slowly she was learning that where God is, fear need not abide. It was an ongoing battle against old habits and inclinations until the day she met her old nemesis face to face.

Friends had told us of a mother (sow) bear in our area that had three cubs with her that spring. Triplets are a little more uncommon than twins, so we hoped we would see them. We took our desires to the Lord during family worship one morning and prayed that the Lord would open up an opportunity for us to see this sow and her cubs.

Of course, Sally added, "safely, Lord." After worship we noticed that there was a bear cub in a small tree just fifteen or so feet from the window. Sure enough, there were two more cubs on the ground with the big sow nearby. As we watched out the window, we could see the sow's nose moving as she analyzed the scents that were reaching her.

"Oh, look," Sally commented, "I bet she smells the waffles cooking." She did! We watched awe-struck as the bear dropped down to all fours and ambled toward the porch. It was a warm spring morning, and the only thing preventing the bear from walking into the house was a thin screen door, which the bear could step right through if it so desired.

Sally, being very practical, moved quickly to the doorway, with the intention to shut the heavy inner door. However, upon reaching the doorway the bear was not there, so Sally opened the screen door to look out and watched as the bear climbed over the porch railing and onto the porch. Nothing prevented the bear from just walking politely up the steps to the porch, but climbing over the rail seemed to suit her better. When you're a bear, few people question your manners.

Sally had stepped back and allowed the screen door to close, but she never got around to shutting the inner door. My two boys and I watched with gaping mouths as she stood there in the doorway while the bear came right up to the door. Sally seemed transfixed as she and the bear stood there, with only a screen door between, evaluating each other.

Then she began to speak. "My, your fur just glistens! You're beautiful!" My wife was sweet-talking a bear! I couldn't believe it, and the bear seemed to enjoy it. Sally went on, admiring everything from the bear's four-inch claws to the large teeth she displayed. Then turning to us she called, "Come, come on over and see her!" We weren't that eager to come closer. After a little bit, the bear dropped down and exited the porch via the railing. She gathered her cubs and set off for whatever bear business was on the agenda that morning.

Suddenly it dawned on Sally what she had done and, turning to me, she exclaimed, "I'm free! I'm free!" So she was! Her old fears were banished. When we talked later, I asked why she had reacted to the bear that way. She told me very matter-of-factly, "Why, the Lord brought the bears. I knew that it was safe." God's grace had delivered her inwardly. She was indeed free! His continued presence had sustained her through her trial. The bears would continue to visit on occasion, providing us the opportunity to develop a lasting friendship with one of her cubs. But that is a bear story for a future book.

For Sally, this experience would forever alter her attitude about the bears. But let me ask you, Did God draw close to us that day and work a miracle? Or had Sally simply become aware of His continual presence with us? Friends, it is our awareness of God's continual presence with us that opens the avenues of the heart to see and understand the mighty workings of God in our behalf.

You see, most of us hold a concept of God in which God sits on His throne in heaven and inclines an ear to us, occasionally altering the events of life in response to our requests. Most of us view God as somewhat aloof, like earthly monarchs who are willing to come to our aid if needed but rarely mingle with the commoners. Visit any surviving kingdom and talk to the subjects, and you will find they feel ill-at-ease with the immediate presence of the royal family.

Likewise, if you were able to read the hearts and thoughts of your fellow humans, you would find that many, if not most, are uncomfortable with the idea of an ever-present God. When one grasps the reality of God as our constant Companion, there is a corresponding change in behavior and attitude. Behavior that might take place outside the context of a king's presence ceases to occur when he is visible. This is after all the normal reaction of a person who has come to an understanding that he is in the presence of one greater than himself. Those who find this environment uncomfortable, who will not uphold a higher standard, will distance themselves from the king.

However much the sinner may wish to avoid God or deny His existence, it is still impossible to hide from God. When Adam and Eve sinned they, in their panic, tried to hide from the Creator. Yet God did not destroy them. He sought them out and continued to love them and care for them. Alcohol, drugs, immorality, materialism, and intellectual denial may dull your senses, but they will never let you do the impossible—hiding from God. The Bible is filled with stories of individuals who tried to run from God: Adam and Eve, Paul, Jonah, just to name a few. All failed miserably to hide from God. It's as the scripture says, "Whither shall I go from thy spirit? or whither shall I flee from thy presence?" (Psalm 139:7).

The Bible says that God is no respecter of persons. This means He doesn't treat some better than others. God does not play favorites. Often people say, "I wish that God would speak to me the way He did back in those old Bible times. Things were easier then."

Friends, it is no harder today! If Enoch, Elijah, and Paul can walk with God, then you can too. If God desires to go through each day with Jim Hohnberger, who is one of the slowest learners and one of the most stubborn men on earth, if God is willing to guide and direct such a man as I with my strong German will and temper, then God desires to be your Companion and Guide too!

If it is so easy, then why do we struggle? Why is it that so few ever find God as a constant Companion? The problem we face is one of attitude. We humans are so used to running our own affairs that we resist the guidance of our loving heavenly Father. We need the attitude of Samuel who said, "Speak, Lord, for thy servant heareth."

This posture is one of complete dependence on a guide who sees and knows that which we do not. It is our lack of willingness to listen to God's voice that denies us His guidance. It is our lack of pliability in obeying His voice that causes the Christian life to be so onerous. We are so used to being in control that even when we attempt to be sensitive to God's Spirit, we tend to discount His leading. The tendency to trust my own knowledge over God's prompting and guiding almost cost me everything beautiful we see about us.

Traveling in New Zealand some years ago, I was a passenger in the front seat of a van. New Zealand is a beautiful country and I was enjoying the sight of the mountains, farms, and sheep. Unexpectedly, I felt the still, small voice of the Spirit prompting me to close my eyes and rest for a little bit. It was only 10:30 in the morning, and I pushed the thought away because, as usual, I thought I knew better than God.

Have you ever reacted the same way to God's guidance? Thankfully, God did not leave me alone when I ignored Him and again the impression came to rest my eyes for a while. Even though I may be a slow learner, I do eventually catch on and remembering past experiences like the log that almost killed me, I was willing to consider this second prompting.

I shut my eyes and laid my head back, still doubtful that there was any purpose for this prompting. BAMM! SMASH! I felt small particles of what had been the windshield moments before shower all over me. A rock had fallen off a nearby hillside and had struck the window directly in front of me. Unlike American antishatter glass, this window shattered into tiny glass fragments that were all through my hair, my ears, down my shirt, even in my nostrils. I sat there and quivered.

I knew that once more the Lord had spared me serious injury. He had saved my eyesight! What a good God we serve! I shuddered at the idea that once again, I had almost ignored His leading. There, with my eyes still shut, I thanked God that I have Him as a constant Companion in my life. I am so very thankful He is not a mere spectator, but with me in all my trials, all my daily activities.

Jesus wants to pilot you and me through our walk on this earth. We can count on Him, because where we are—God is!

When a person becomes convinced that God is ever present with them, then it is that God can perform great miracles for them. So it was for the three Hebrew captives described in Daniel chapter 3. They had been summoned to appear at the dedication of a great golden image that Nebuchadnezzar had set up. All were expected to bow before this image of the king and everyone did except Shadrach, Meshach, and Abednego. The king was enraged at what he considered open defiance and threatened them with a hellish death if they refused to obey. They would be bound and tossed into a fiery furnace to die in the flames as an example to all of what happens to those who refuse to obey the king.

They calmly replied, "Our God whom we serve is able to deliver us from the burning fiery furnace, and he will deliver us out of thine hand, O king" (Daniel 3:17). There was no despair at the situation they found themselves in, no faithless timidity, just a quiet, total confidence that God would be with them. King Nebuchadnezzar was so angered by their response that he ordered the furnace made hotter than ever and had the three young men thrown in. It was a brash action prompted by an out-of-control temper used to having its own way, and it cost him several of his strongest soldiers, who died from the heat as they tossed the captives into the furnace.

The king did not have long to enjoy his triumph over these defiant Hebrews. Upon glancing in the furnace he exclaimed, "Lo, I see four men loose, walking in the midst of the fire, and they have no hurt; and the form of the fourth is like the Son of God" (Daniel 3:25). When the crisis came, God was there at their side, a visible presence to encourage, guide, and protect. He had been there all along. Heaven is no further away today than it was then, but God can do little for us when we lose a sense of our constant dependence on Him.

The story of the three Hebrews is a vivid demonstration of what the life of faith is all about. They were ever dependent upon a power outside of themselves and constantly yielded to the still, small voice of the One who walked with them.

While writing this book, I experienced the power of an ever-present God and His protecting hand. It had been a wet fall with day after day of heavy rain. The ground was saturated. The night before Sally and I were to fly to Dallas, Texas for some meetings, the rain changed to snow and by early morning there was an inch of snow on the ground. Unfortunately, with so much water on the gravel road, it froze into a slippery mass of ice and stone.

Living in the wilderness makes it necessary to leave our house in the predawn hours to make our morning flights. This particular morning found us on the road at 4:30 in the morning. Driving down that familiar wilderness road that leads toward civilization we came to a sharp, horseshoe-shaped, descending curve and started to slide. However, when you start to slide in a four-wheel-drive vehicle with antilock brakes, you don't slide to one side or the other, but rather the vehicle slides straight forward without any vestige of control.

Unfortunately, at this point in the road, straight ahead meant a rather intimate acquaintance with some large cottonwood trees. If we managed to miss those trees, we would fare no better, for the hillside at this point was so steeply angled that we would no doubt only travel a short distance before our Ford Explorer would roll 360 degrees all the way to the creek below.

I could picture in my mind's eye the jarring impact with those trees and the instantaneous airbag deployment. I called out, "LORD, NO!" and then we left the road at forty miles per hour.

Suddenly we stopped. The Explorer rested well off the road on a steep hillside. Those cottonwood trees were only inches from Sally's door. Stepping gingerly out of the vehicle, I took a flashlight and examined our position. The truck was so sharply angled that one wheel was actually off the ground.

Walking back up to the road, I examined our tire tracks and could not humanly explain our good fortune. The tire tracks were headed directly toward the trees and yet something or someone had pushed us aside at the last possible moment. There was no natural obstacle, the slope should have pushed us even more solidly into the trees, but an ever-present God had saved us. Hours later when the wrecker from town managed to save our truck by winching it sideways away from the trees, we found there wasn't even a scratch on the vehicle.

All of us, myself included, need to pray for and cultivate an increasing awareness, a more perfect consciousness of God's presence with us. Then we will be more likely to respond to His overtures and guidance. When we are aware of His presence, our hearts will commune more readily with Him and come to know Him in ever-increasing degrees. Our cooperation will become more perfect through faith, love, and practice. However, it will require a lot of courage to wrench us loose from the grip of our times.

One of the most endearing terms for Jesus in all of Scripture is Immanuel, which means "God with us." We need to learn that God is not in some far removed heavenly place, occasionally looking down on us. No, when Jesus left earth He promised to send the Comforter, God's Spirit, that He might be always with us. Now, that is a comfort to me. Today I no longer pray to a God in some distant place, but I recognize Him as my constant Companion. And He is!

CHAPTER 6

Seeing Him Who Is Invisible

"For he endured, as seeing him who is invisible" (Hebrews 11:27).

After the Battle of Gettysburg, General Robert E. Lee happened upon an officer who was analyzing some of the mistakes of Gettysburg.

"Young man," responded Lee, "why did you not tell me that before the battle? Even as stupid a man as I am can see it all now."

Most of us accept Lee's premise that 20/20 hindsight is an inevitable part of life, but still there are those memories. Uncomfortable memories of what might have been . . . if only. If only we could have known then what we know now. Who among us can look back at their life's history without a twinge of pain at the mistakes made or feelings of regret over the foolish errors in judgment, the missed blessings, the lost opportunities? Even as you read these lines, the moments pass one by one into eternity, etching as they go a record which we will look back on in the future. Will your future history be as full of regrets as your past has been?

Friends, I wish there were a way I could show you a movie of my life as a Christian. No one ever taught me these things that I am sharing with you. It took me years—literally years—of trial and error and many mistakes to figure each one of these principles out for myself.

By now you understand I was not satisfied with a simply intellectual knowledge, but rather I desired truth that had a practical application to my life. I hope I can ignite that same desire within your soul. That excites me, for religion apart from practical, daily—in fact, moment by moment—application to the life is nearly useless.

In the early days of the Christian church, our religion was strong and vital. It changed lives so completely that people stood in awe. It was a religion with power.

It is here that the churches of our day have failed their membership and violated the very reason for their existence. Why is it that the churches, all the Christian churches, have so many new converts turn from them in disgust? Why is it that so few of the youth in the churches ever seem to hold on to the faith? Why is it that religion makes only minimal differences in the divorce rates among Christian couples as compared to the world? Have you ever stopped to honestly ask yourself these questions?

Church leaders have, and their answers have spawned a slew of programs in the church designed to address these areas of weakness. Almost every one of them is a dismal failure! Why? Because they attempt to deal with the symptoms rather than the problem. The great plague in Christianity is that few—very, very few—of those who claim to be Christians (very, very few even among those who are ministers), possess a gospel capable of transforming their whole life.

That was a bold statement. So let me demonstrate:

Once I was invited to speak to a group of ministers. I am just a lay preacher, not a professional minister. What should I say when addressing the "experts"? As I stood at that podium, I said, "I wish that every time a minister stood in the pulpit, a big screen would come down behind him and show how he led his life in the preceding week—how he acted in his home with his children and his wife, how he responded to temptations and trials. Would you get up and preach if those were the conditions?"

"NO!" the ministers responded.

"Then my friends, you have not found the gospel. Jesus would have had no problem with such a condition. He knew His actions were just as straight and pure as His doctrines."

The history of the early church is recorded biblically in the book Acts of the Apostles. Actions—not doctrines of the Apostles, not beliefs of the Apostles, not sermons of the Apostles, but actions—these are the mark of the true gospel. For it is "by their fruits [that] ye shall know them."

Dear reader, would you be willing to be put under such scrutiny? If not, then I challenge you to do something different with this book than you have done with any other book you have read. What you hold in your hands is a workbook for a project that you are going to build in your own life. It is up to you, the reader, to take the experiences here described and make them part of your experience. Take the thoughts presented and mull them over, chew on them, assimilate them in a practical way, until they become your own.

It requires very little for you to live a life like this. You need only to cultivate a sense of God's presence with you throughout the day and then you must be motivated to act on His guidance. Too simple? Watch and see.

I got a phone call one evening from a man I had met several years before. He and his family had visited us to see our wilderness property and our lifestyle. We shared with them about the practical gospel we were applying to our lives, but they just weren't that interested. Now he was on the phone saying, "Jim, I'd like your family to come to our place for a weekend. I know you have come to understand the practical gospel and we need a little help with the family and the marriage." I told him I would pray about it. Afterward, feeling that I had the Lord's permission to do so, I called Rob back and we set up a date to visit them.

Arriving on a Friday evening, Rob wanted me to go for a walk with him. You see, Rob hadn't told me the whole story. He hadn't had what a lawyer might call "full disclosure." It turned out that just prior to his call to me, Rob's wife had told him that she was finished with him. She wasn't mad at him. It was just over. There were no feelings left. She planned to leave him and take the children. Rob asked her if she would stay if he really changed. She consented that if he would really change, then she would consider staying. So Rob had a week-end in which to change if he wanted to save his marriage.

"Rob," I said once the whole story had come out, "the God I have come to know in the mountains—His gospel is so powerful I guarantee that you can be a new creature in Christ by Sunday. But, Rob," I continued "I cannot guarantee that your wife won't leave you."

"Well, what do I do?" he asked

"Simply take this one text and apply it to your life. It is found in James 1:19: 'Let every man be swift to hear, slow to speak, slow to wrath.'"

Rob looked at me like "So?!" It was almost as if he said, "I've read that lots of times, and THAT is supposed to save my marriage?!"

Well, that's just the problem many of us have with the Scriptures. We read them and go on our way, never stopping to think about what it means in a practical application to our lives.

I went on. "Rob, what does it mean 'let every man be swift to hear'? It means that you are going to have to cultivate a sensitivity to hear the voice of God, an awareness of God's presence with you throughout the day. For the first time in your life, you're going to have to let someone else guide your actions. You are going to have to learn to take each situation and filter what you know and see through the unseen God who knows that which you do not.

"Everything in this world is designed to intrude upon faith in an invisible God. The visible world is the enemy of the invisible God. The visible world clamors for your attention, intrudes upon your senses, and insists that you listen to it. You will have to break this habit and instead listen to the voice of God, 'And thine ears shall hear a word behind thee, saying, This is the way, walk ye in it' (Isaiah 30:21).

"Now Rob, what about that 'slow to speak'? It means that we filter our every word through God that He may guide us."

Rob had not been in the habit of filtering his words. In fact, that was one of the main reasons he was in such trouble with his wife. I could relate—I had been there—but now I could speak from the perspective of having seen the difference this filtering process made.

I remember one morning I had been working in the garage cleaning and sharpening one of my chain saws. After filling it with gas and oil, I returned it to its proper place ready for use in the future. I enjoy working with my hands, but I dislike the smell of petroleum products on my skin so before I started a new project, I walked to the back door of the cabin that is close to a bathroom where I could wash my hands.

Lathering my hands, I was happy and having a good day with the Lord. "Whatcha doing, dear?" a sweet voice queried from the doorway.

I glanced up to see Sally looking in on me. Immediately I could feel my flesh want to rise up and say, "What do you mean? Can't you see I'm washing my hands? That's a stupid question!" In the past I would have said all that and more. My marriage would have suffered. But while my flesh was rising, I could hear the quiet voice of God saying, *Treat her gently, Jim.* Which voice am I going to listen to, the voice of the flesh that wants to complain about her silly question or the voice of God? I am so thankful I chose to say, "Washing my hands, dear."

"That's fine, honey. I was just wondering how your day was going," my sweet wife responded, the harmony between us unbroken.

Men, why is it that after we marry our wives, we want them to do everything and phrase everything exactly like we would? We need to understand that in our wives, the Lord has brought a beautiful difference and balance into our lives. I wouldn't have phrased the inquiry the same way she did, but the very reason I was attracted to my wife was that she thinks, acts, looks, and even smells different than Jim Hohnberger. That, gentlemen, is good news!

So, I want all you men to know that my marriage—more importantly my attitude toward the wonderful person I am married to—

improved drastically once I recognized and learned to treasure these differences. If you want to improve your marriage, learn to cultivate a sense of God's presence with you, and respond to it. It works, every time, but Rob had yet to discover this.

"Now Rob, let's look at the last part of the text," I continued. " 'Slow to wrath' means that even when our wives and children provoke us, we choose to remain in Christ and let His sweet Spirit control us rather than the passions of the moment, as we have too often let them in the past. We choose to surrender these upset feelings to God and allow Him to remove them from our lives before they damage the ones we love."

Rob and I had been on a long walk by this time—a walk punctuated by more than a few tears. He went to bed that night with a lot to think about! And so began one of the most extraordinary weekends I have ever experienced.

When we awoke the next day, I wondered how it would go. I prayed for this couple no human could help, but with whom the Almighty was striving. There was a beautiful breakfast spread before us this morning, and as we sat at the table, I noticed a large dish of steaming oatmeal in front of Rob. As soon as the blessing was said, Rob stood and began to serve himself the oatmeal. The self-serving, me-first attitude just seemed to flow from him.

I sat there wondering if Rod had considered filtering his actions through God when suddenly, he stopped what he was doing, paused for just a moment and then handed the bowl to my son. He then served my other son, my wife, me, and then his wife and his children. As he did this, I ventured a glance at his wife. She was staring open-mouthed at her husband. You know, I truly believe that in their entire marriage, this was the first time she had ever seen Rob serve anyone but himself first. Rob was becoming swift to hear. The Spirit of the Lord was manifesting Himself to Rob's consciousness and Rob was beginning to cooperate with Him who is invisible.

A little later on in the meal, his five-year-old daughter who was used to running the household, rudely—and I mean rudely—interrupted her father while he was speaking. Remember what Rob and I had talked about the night before, being slow to speak and slow to wrath? Well, this certainly wasn't Rob's natural inclination and he demonstrated it by responding to his daughter in harshness and anger.

Then he abruptly fell silent. I have never seen someone do what he did next, but he just bowed his head right there in front of us all for a moment and when he looked up at his daughter, it was in the Spirit of God and everyone there could see the difference. Again I looked at his wife and found her astonished at the changes in her "hopeless" husband. I was sitting there watching this and even I could hardly believe the contrast.

I was seeing this man's life transformed before my very eyes! The invisible God was guiding and instructing this failure of a husband and by allowing that process, Rob was working out his salvation with fear and trembling. "For it is God which worketh in you both to will and to do of his good pleasure" (Philippians 2:12-13).

I wish I could take time to share the whole weekend with you because it continued like that. It was marvelous! Finally during a discussion near the end of the weekend, Rob had an opportunity to deliver one of those zingers to his wife. You know, just a cute little sarcasm at which everybody laughs, but the wife aches and cries inside because she's been jabbed.

When this goes on year after year, finally she becomes so hardened that there are just no feelings left and she wants a divorce. In the silence that followed his inconsiderate jab, Rob looked at his wife and in a moment of honesty exclaimed, "Why do I do this to you? I have been doing this to you all the years of our married life. Will you forgive me?" You could just see the remorse and self-loathing on his face. There were tears in her eyes, for finally, she was a prisoner of hope.

Sunday afternoon, just we four adults gathered alone. I wanted to know what she would do. Would she leave him? No, she had decided she wouldn't.

"Finally I see a little glimmer of hope that maybe this thing can work out," she responded. We left them with bright hope for the future but also the knowledge of how easily Satan can derail a new experience.

Hope is all many of us want, just a glimmer of hope that things can work out, whether our problem is a marriage gone bad or being a single parent, or something totally different.

Moses had problems too. He was charged with leading a whole nation of Jim Hohnbergers to the Promised Land. A whole nation of stubborn, self-willed individuals. I wouldn't wish that job on anybody! But Moses "endured, as seeing Him who is invisible." He learned to view the visible—the lack of food, the absence of water, the rebellions, the snakes, the idolatry—through the eyes of the invisible God. When he did this, all problems sank in obscurity. Nothing was too hard for God! If we would cultivate this skill and trust in Him who knows and sees all, we would see more of God's hand in the providences of our lives.

After more than two years in the wilderness, I knew I would have to eventually find some type of employment, but as of yet, it was not clear what I should do. I believed that my all-knowing heavenly Father knew what I should do. However, this was early on in my experience and I had a hard time following His leading. God had to be persistent to get my attention.

While doing some errands in town, I happened to run into the owner of the local real estate office. We had worked with Paul when we first contemplated moving to Montana. Even though he had been unable to help us, he was a typically friendly westerner and greeted me warmly. Then he said, "You know, I've been thinking about you lately. I'm considering expanding my office's dealing in rural and wilderness property and I think you should come work for me."

I thanked him, but turned the idea down. After all, I had spent most of my life in sales and I knew that selling real estate would require me to spend time in the office and go to sales meetings. I would have to get a license and I couldn't sell property without a phone. At that time, the only phone service in our valley was radio-telephone and this was so cost prohibitive that there was no sense in even considering it.

But the idea wouldn't go away, and soon it seemed that every time I went to town I would see Paul, in a store or on the street and always he encouraged me to consider working for him. Finally I agreed to meet with him and discuss the possibilities. I was still sure that it was a waste of time, but it was becoming clear that Paul would not be denied until I was able to demonstrate to him just how impractical this idea was.

Soon I found myself seated with Sally across from Paul in his office. "So, what is it going to take to get you to come work for me, Jim?"

"Well," I began, "I am not licensed. You would have to pay all my expenses to become licensed, including my books and examination fees." Paul just nodded, so I continued. "When I came up to the mountains, I worked very hard to get control of my time. If I am going to come on board, you must promise me that I will never be required to attend any meetings. I must be allowed to work just as much or as little as I desire. You would also have to pay any association fees and cover all my advertising costs."

"Is that all you want, Jim?"

"No. You will have to set up and pay for all the expenses related to a radio-telephone line at my house."

"Is that it?" he asked.

"Yes," I responded.

"Great!" With scarcely concealed triumph, he reached into his desk drawer, pulled out two books and handed them over to me. I found myself holding the study guides for the licensing exam.

"You're crazy," I finally managed to blurt out. I had offered him the worst deal in the world. No businessman would lay out that kind of money with no guarantee of a return.

Paul just smiled at me and said, "Let me know when you're ready to take the exam." Only later would I find out that Paul had checked me out with some business associates in Wisconsin.

They told him, "Jim Hohnberger does his best work by himself. You just leave him alone, and he'll do fine."

Belatedly realizing that God had been altering events and trying to get my attention, I decided the only avenue open to me was to approach real estate sales in the same manner I was trying to approach my whole life, which was "Lord, what would Thou have me to do?" So when I met with a client, I would appeal to the Lord to guide me in my choice of property to show them and the Lord blessed my dependence upon Him.

I told Paul he was crazy, but was he? Soon I was the number one grossing agent in the office and our office became first in the state. To think, I had nearly discarded the idea of selling real estate. Independence from God has always been the curse of Jim Hohnberger's life. I am learning day by day to become less and less trustful of self and I pray that the Lord will make me more sensitive to His Spirit's leading. Unfortunately, I am such a slow learner that I sometimes despair that I will ever learn. You see, God desires to guide each of us on the pathway of life, but sometimes His guidance doesn't seem to make sense to us, except in hindsight.

"Jim, will you go up to the greenhouse and close it up for the night before you go on your walk?" Sally asked me one evening.

"Sure," I said heading up the hill to the greenhouse. The greenhouse must be ventilated on warm days to keep it from overheating. However, nights in the mountains can be chilly even in summer so the vents must be closed to protect the tender plants. It was six in the evening when I finished shutting things up for the night. I usually take a short walk by the river in the evening. This helps me unwind and relax before our family time at 6:30. Tonight I changed my mind and decided to walk along the back edge of our property rather than going down by the river.

Setting out, I felt the following impression upon my mind, *Jim, you need to tell your wife where you are going. You might be mauled by a grizzly bear.* This seemed a little silly. After all, I was within sight of my house. So I reasoned it away. Again the same impression came and again I pushed it aside, but I was uneasy and still wrestling with it in my mind.

After walking about two hundred yards, I came to a sharp little drop in elevation on my property known as a bench. Just as I started down this incline, I felt a chill that had nothing to do with the weather.

Looking about, I saw a female grizzly bear with cubs. She was standing up on her haunches thirty or forty feet to my left and staring right at me. Now when a bear stares at you, they don't just stand there and stare. Because they don't see really well, they shift a little back and forth trying to focus and sort of look right through you. It is about the most disconcerting and frightening experience you can imagine.

Looking at that bear, the Bible story of Elisha and the disrespectful boys whom God punished with two she-bears raced through my mind. Those two bears spanked, so to speak, forty-two boys. I couldn't help but wonder if I was about to be spanked for failing to listen to that still, small voice of God's Spirit.

I looked around at the trees nearby and thought to myself, *there is no way I could make it!* Besides, I intuitively knew that I had to approach this visible problem through the power of the invisible.

Jesus said, "My sheep hear my voice, and I know them, and they follow me" (John 10:27). I realized that it was not enough to know that God was speaking to me. It was not enough to recognize His desire to lead in my life. I had to follow Him and it was here that I had failed. I prayed, "Lord, forgive me! What would You have me to do, now?"

Duck down Jim, below the level of the bench so she can't see you, then go FAST to the guest cabin. This was the impression I had, so I dropped down to the bottom of the bench and began to move quickly toward the guest cabin. But even at this point, I didn't fully obey. Thank God He doesn't abandon us just because we fail to listen. What a long-suffering God we serve!

My mother has always told me "Jim, that curiosity of yours is going to get you in big trouble someday." Well, as I was running along the bottom of that little hill I wondered what the bear was doing. After all, nothing was biting at my rear end as I ran. In obeying the impression to go to the guesthouse, I had turned my back on the bear and I hate having my back to a grizzly.

I was about halfway to the guesthouse when I spotted a stump up on top of the bench and I decided that I would climb up there on that stump and check out what the bear was doing. Looking back, I found she wasn't where I expected her to be. The place she had been was empty except for her cubs, which she had sent up a tree. They were just squalling away in that Douglas Fir tree, but they stayed out of Mom's way while she dealt with me.

Glancing about, I saw her standing up on her haunches in the place I had just left, and she was looking right at me. I knew bears well enough by this point to know she was going to charge me. She heard her cubs crying in that tree, and the fire in her eyes told me she was not pleased with Jim Hohnberger! I looked at the guesthouse and I told myself, "There is no way I can make it there!"

Do you have any idea how fast a grizzly bear can run? They run a lot faster than Jim Hohnberger, even with a lot of adrenaline in his system! Palms 34:6 says, "This poor man cried, and the Lord heard him, and saved him out of all his troubles." Now that's the kind of God I want to serve! Don't you? A God who saves those who cry unto Him.

In distress and self-disgust, I prayed, "Lord, will I **EVER** learn!"
Just hold still, Jim. You'll be OK.

As I watched, the bear dropped down to all fours and grunted for her cubs. At least they knew how to obey and came running. It was only June, and they were still very young, little more than two balls of fluff, but by the end of the summer they would be well on their way to becoming predators just as fearsome as their mother. With her cubs by her side once more, the bear turned to me and snorted her disgust before ambling off into the woods.

Learning to break the habit of ignoring the invisible presence of the Lord can only be done through the medium of faith. Each of us needs to develop a spiritual awareness until it becomes the most important thing in our lives, the thing to which we cling for direction.

I'm not the only one who heads for trouble when I lose the perspective of an ever-present God. My family suffers too. It has always been this way from the moment sin entered the world. When Eve came to Adam with the forbidden fruit, he knew she had disobeyed God. Yet Adam thought that he loved Eve so much that the very idea of separation was impossible to contemplate. He chose to eat of the fruit in order to remain with her, even if their only future together was death. Watch how his attitude changes now that his will and ways are not surrendered to God.

When confronted with his own actions, Adam blames Eve, and then blames God for creating her! "The woman whom thou gavest to be with me, she gave me of the tree, and I did eat" (Genesis 3:12). I have found that it is usually my spouse that bears the brunt of my frustration when I lose sight of the presence of God with me. However, I have also found that nothing has so improved my marriage as learning to filter "the seen," my words and actions, through the influence of the "unseen," God.

Things have changed a lot in the years since I started selling wilderness real estate. I work exclusively for God now, speaking and writing, sharing those things He has taught me. Our family gets invited to speak about the gospel in many different locations all over the globe.

We had just flown home after sixty days in Australia and New Zealand, where met many wonderful people and ministered to their needs. We often stay with the families that invite us and we had not eaten a meal by ourselves—just the four of us—in those sixty days. We flew into Kalispell, Montana, exhausted. We felt like towels that had been put through an old-fashioned wringer washing machine. All the energy had been wrung out, and we longed for solitude and the simple pleasure of a meal in privacy.

Heading up the North Fork Road, we found over two feet of snow on the ground. With the truck in four-wheel drive, we drove home and into our driveway. By this time, the snow was so deep the truck was pushing it out in front of us. Pulling up to the house, I asked Sally to go in and start the wood stove and prepare a simple meal.

"Matthew," I said, "I will unload the car if you will take the things I bring in and put them away." He agreed, and lastly I asked Andrew to go to the garage and get the snow blower out and clear the snow from the walkways and the area around the garage. Everyone went about their jobs, and soon the pleasant smell of food greeted me whenever I stepped into the house with belongings from the car.

Many hands make light work, and again this proved to be true. The car was empty, and I stepped outside to check under the seats and make sure I didn't forget anything. I could see Andrew over by the garage finishing up with the snow blower and getting ready to put it away. I have trained my boys that tools should not be put away dirty but rather should be put away in such a manner that they are ready for use. This means that we refuel things like the chain saws and fill them with oil. It means that we take a broom and sweep all the snow out of the snow blower before we put it in the garage.

True to his training, Andrew got the very expensive Fuller Brush broom to clean the snow blower. The machine was still running and it seemed to him that he could just jam the broom in quickly and jerk it back out to knock the snow loose. This would save him the effort of shutting down the engine and starting it all over again just to drive it into the garage. Like the rest of us, he was exhausted from our sixty days' effort.

I was busy feeling under the seat when I heard the terrible clatter of metal against metal. I didn't have to even raise my head to know what had happened. When I did look, I saw that the tines had grabbed the broom and twisted it until the metal handle looked like a corkscrew. Andrew was down on his knees trying to extract the broom. I found myself walking quickly toward my son with words of rebuke on the tip of my tongue. When I stood by him, he wouldn't look up at me. He was, perhaps, fearful of my reaction.

Think about it for a minute. We had just returned from preaching the practical gospel on the other side of the world and he was concerned, and rightly so, about his father's reaction. I am so thankful that he didn't look up right away. It gave me a few blessed moments to hear the voice of God say *Jim, have you asked Me what I'd have you to do?*

"Well no, Lord. I know what he did wrong and I thought I would give him a little lecture so he will learn from this mistake," I said, excusing myself.

Just smile at him, Jim.

"Just smile?! You have got to be kidding, Lord! Why, that was my expensive broom he just ruined!"

Just smile, Jim. The natural consequences are sufficient. Of course, this all happened in a fraction of a second. It takes longer to read than it did to occur. Andrew looked up at this point and I smiled at him and said, "Come on. Let's go eat."

Later at the table as we were eating, Andrew said, "Father?"

"Yes, Son."

"I'm sorry. It was a stupid thing to do."

You know, we have all done foolish things in our lives. The Lord was right. The natural consequences of his action were sufficient to prevent any reoccurrence. Andrew would never do something like that again. If I had lectured as my flesh wanted to, the lesson might well have been lost. His focus could easily have become defending himself against Father's wrath rather than learning self-government. What would Andrew have thought of the gospel I believe and had preached for sixty days, if it had been unable to keep me from uttering words I would have regretted? I know what he would have concluded and he would have been right! "If any man among you seem to be religious, and bridleth not his tongue, . . . this man's religion is vain" (James 1:26).

That is the problem in Christianity today. Most youth see that their parents' religion, behind closed doors, is vain, and when they are old enough, they walk away from such useless religion. I'm told that some denominations are losing 75 percent of their youth. It shouldn't surprise us, because we haven't learned to recognize God's invisible presence with us and to yield to His gentle entreaties. God desires us to apply these principles in all our interpersonal relationships, be it with friends or strangers that we meet on the street, but does that include those who do not treat us kindly? I leave you to judge.

When one lives up in the mountains, a four-wheel drive is not a luxury, not a fashionable vehicle of suburban mothers, but an absolute necessity if one must be mobile in the winter. I have to depend on the vehicle not to strand my wife or family in the wilderness, so I am sensitive to the mechanical needs of my vehicle.

When it was time to replace my Toyota Land Cruiser, I went into town and purchased a new sport utility vehicle. Shortly after I purchased it, I started hearing a sound from one of my front hubs. It was not a good sound to hear coming from a four-wheel drive, so I took it to the dealer, and they gladly replaced the hub as the truck was still under warranty. Towards the end of the warranty, I noticed the same type of sound starting to come from the other front hub. Knowing what was wrong this time, I made an appointment to have it examined at the dealer where I purchased the truck.

You must understand that it is a weakness in my character to become irritated when things go wrong. Realizing this, I go to great lengths to make sure that things run smoothly. This way, I help to decrease temptations to lose self-control and become irritated. With this in mind, I made my appointment at the dealership the very first one of the day at 8:00 A.M. I explained the problem to Brent, the assistant service manager and asked him how long he felt it would take.

"About an hour," he responded.

I decided to take a walk around town and do a few little errands. I planned my morning so I would not arrive back at the dealership until 9:15 A.M. That way I was sure the car would be done and I would have no opportunity to become frustrated because it wasn't ready.

When I returned to pick up my car, I noticed it was still in the same place I had left it. It was possible that it had been parked there after servicing, but it made me a little uneasy, and with a sense of foreboding I entered the service department. "Is it all set?" I asked Brent as I came up to the counter.

"Haven't had a chance to bring it in," He responded.

I could feel the frustration building in my flesh. "When do you think you will be able to look at it?"

"I'm not sure. I really don't think it's a problem, Jim."

Again I could feel the frustration level rise. I wanted to straighten him out and defend my rights. Thankfully the Lord is an ever-present help in time of danger, and I was in danger, not from the service manager, but from my own flesh, which wanted to have control of me right then.

Surrender it to Me, the Lord whispered in my thoughts.

All right, Lord, You can have this frustration. "Brent," I asked in a reasonable voice, "how would you know there is nothing wrong if you haven't even looked at it? Would you at least consent to take it out and drive it? The noise is unmistakable." He grudgingly agreed to drive it and was back in a very short time.

"I don't think it's anything," he said matter-of-factly.

"Didn't you hear the noise?" I asked.

"Yeah, I heard it. I think it is just the fact that it is in four-wheel drive on the dry pavement rather than the snow where there would be a little slipping."

This was the strangest explanation I had ever heard. "But it is the same sound the other side made when it was bad," I pleaded.

"No, it's different."

Lord, this isn't fair! He has prejudged the situation and isn't even being reasonable.

Just stay in Me, Jim. You don't have to let go of Me regardless of how others may act toward you.

"Brent, if you change the hub and the noise went away, wouldn't you agree that that was the problem?" I asked.

"No," he responded.

"No, you wouldn't change the hub, or no, you wouldn't agree that that was the problem?"

"I wouldn't agree to either," Brent said, becoming irritated.

"Well, Brent, I can't make you change the hub."

"No, you can't," he agreed forcibly.

"Brent, I am scheduled to leave for Europe next week and my wife is going to be here alone, with this truck. I'm sure it is the same thing as the other hub. Besides, by the time I return the truck will be off warranty."

"That's your problem!" he responded.

"We just don't agree, do we?" I asked.

"No, we don't."

"I guess all I can do is take it home and bring it back in if it gets worse."

"I guess so," he said. "You can pay over there," he commented, handing me a bill.

I walked toward the cashiers desk with a sinking feeling in my heart. *Lord,* I prayed silently, *I have never been treated so unfairly in all my life and now I am supposed to pay for it too. This is just too much!*

Trust in Me, Jim and surrender it all to Me.

Oh, it is so hard when we feel our rights have been trampled and our flesh wants to straighten out the wrongs that have been done to us.

I didn't know it, but Sam, the service manager, had been watching all of this transpire, and at this point he approached me. "Jim, are you uncomfortable with the decision that was rendered?"

"Am I ever!" I told him, explaining the whole situation.

"If I bring it in and change the hub and the noise doesn't go away, are you willing to pay for the labor of putting it on and taking it back off?"

"Certainly," I replied. "But if the sound does go away, are you willing to agree that the hub was the problem and cover it under the warranty?"

Sam agreed, and the truck was brought in. The hub was replaced, and the sound vanished! God had the situation in hand and had a solution there for me all the time. I didn't need to defend myself when the God of the universe was at my side. I simply needed to surrender to Him.

Do you, right now, sense the invisible presence of God calling to your heart? He wants to be your present Helper. "And thine ears shall hear a word behind thee, saying, This is the way, walk ye in it" (Isaiah 30:21). He wants to empower you to live above the pull of the flesh, above the pull of the world. It is when the world sees us being saved in the present rather than just saved from our past that our lives will demonstrate that we have the power of God rather than just a form of godliness. Today's churches for the most part have lost this power, and this is the reason many turn from them. People long for a power able to save them from themselves, a power that makes life here a joy. They desire more than just lame promises of joy in the hereafter.

This experience is within the reach of all. It wasn't until I purposed in my heart daily, hourly, moment by moment to cooperate with the invisible God that my experience blossomed. Today, it continues to flower and produce fruit as I address the visible through the invisible God. I am not writing as one who has arrived, nor experienced to the fullest the opportunity that awaits us, but as one who is pressing on. "While we look not at the things which are seen, but at the things which are not seen: for the things which are seen are temporal; but the things which are not seen are eternal" (2 Corinthians 4:18).

When I first began to see and understand this experience I would pray daily, "Lord help me be so sensitive to Your presence that the lightest whisper of Jesus will move my soul." Now, I can write as one who is experiencing the deeper life and maturing in it. And I'm not the only one. As I travel the globe there are a few here and there who are willing to put forth the effort to make this experience theirs.

Many desire it, but because it involves continual self-denial, few seem to find it. It breaks my heart because they come so close, they examine the experience, they feel the pull of the heart for oneness with God. They see that God has been in pursuit of them their whole life, and they understand the lifestyle changes they should implement to make surrender to God easier. They realize that all their choices must be submitted to Him, and they recognize that God is always with us to lead and direct, if we are willing to follow. But they never change. It has been an intellectual exercise, rather than an affair of the heart. Don't let this happen to you. Rob had been motivated to make this experience real because he was in danger of losing his whole family, but many more are in the same type of danger and do not realize it. What is it going to take to motivate you?

Two weeks after our visit with Rob's family I began to wonder how things were going for them. Had Rob fallen back into his old ways, or was he keeping an awareness of God's presence and submitting to His guidance?

Then Rob called. "Jim, my wife has become my best friend! You will never believe it, but my wife and I have stayed up every night for the last two weeks talking until late at night. You know, she has something to say. I never knew it. I never gave her the chance. I want to thank you," he said. "I also want you to know that you are free to use our story to help others see and believe. I didn't know my wife was thinking about leaving. I really didn't know, and if I didn't know it, then there are other men out there whose wives are thinking about it too."

Rob spoke of the risk of temporal loss, but far worse would be the loss of your spouse or your children to the heavenly kingdom. Do you really believe that they can rise to a higher level of spiritual existence than you yourself practice? Are they worth the effort? Christ thought we were worth that effort for He said, "For their sakes I sanctify Myself." Shouldn't we do the same for those we love?

Rob was slowly learning in every situation of life to see Him who is invisible and be guided by Him. You and I can possess this experience too, but we are so used to following inclination, impulse, and reacting to the visible world about us that it will take some retraining to hear the voice of God and to sense His presence in every situation. Above the chaos of the world, beyond the clamor of emotions, greater than our intellectual knowledge, is the quiet presence of God awaiting only our recognition and cooperation, that He may guide, comfort, and direct us. This is the key to a life without regrets.

CHAPTER 7

Selective Hearing

"Speak, Lord; for thy servant heareth"
(1 Samuel 3:9).

"My hands slid along the rope as my feet took slow, tentative steps. They were so slow that my five-year-old guide could easily outpace me. With each step came an awareness that I had entered a world where darkness reigned and hearing was the most precious of senses." I found myself drawn into the experience as my friend told me of the unique trail he and his wife hiked blindfolded.

"My hands were chilly in the forty degree weather," he stated, "but I resisted the urge to pull on my gloves for fear of losing even more sensory input. My hands, more than my feet, told of passing distance as the guide rope slid gently through them. An occasional knot announced the completion of another rope length. Turns could only be sensed from the angle changes in the rope.

"The scents of raw earth so recently exposed by the melting snows accompanied me as I walked and the sweet smell of cedar announced their presence along the trail. Most of the odors were warm and friendly until I caught the scent of carrion. It's probably a dead deer, I thought. The odor was strong, and I realized the carcass was very nearby. It made me nervous that perhaps we might startle a bear awakened by the warm spell and drawn to the smell of death.

"As I walked I became increasingly dependent upon my ears. The crunch of snow underfoot warned me of slippery conditions. The gurgling sound of a mountain brook growing closer by the moment set me to wondering if I would accidentally step into the icy water. But by far, the most reassuring sound was the voice of my son, who at five years of age was acting as my guide. 'There is more snow here, Daddy,' or 'Watch out for this stump!' he warned. I smiled inwardly, thinking I can't 'watch out' for anything. Then suddenly I ran into him. He intentionally placed himself in front of the stump to protect me from danger. My utter dependence upon him was awkward and scary.

"Sometimes we walked in silence, and after a little while I feared that he had moved on ahead and left me to struggle alone with the unseen obstacles. I called out, only to find he was right beside me. 'Please don't leave me,' I said pleadingly. Without his eyes I could only grope my way along the guide line. With his vision I could walk, confident that he would warn and protect me from danger. 'Oh Daddy, I would never leave you!' he exclaimed, incredulous that I could even contemplate such a thought.

"At length I came to the end of the rope, the end of my journey. I removed my blindfold, only to be dazzled by the light of day. After I adjusted and could focus once more, I saw the smiling face of my guide beaming up at me, serene in the confidence that he could see me through."

God wants to guide you and me in exactly the same way. We may have little confidence in Him. We probably have never trusted Him completely with our whole lives. Maybe we haven't even known personally anyone who trusted God that completely. Yet, He is not offended. He knows that by our very nature, we are inclined to refuse His guidance. And still God stands ready to assist, confident just like that little boy that He can do the job.

You see, God knows all the problems, all the heartaches that we will face in this life and He has a solution for every one of them. Better, far better than just a solution to our problems is the fact that the God of the universe is in sympathy with our struggles.

The Bible says, "For we have not an high priest which cannot be touched with the feeling of our infirmities; but was in all points tempted like as we are" (Hebrews 4:15).

That is good news! Jesus knows what we are going through. He knows how we feel, how tired we become, and He understands the heartaches that not even the closest human friend can share. Just like that five-year-old guide, He says, "I will never leave thee, nor forsake thee" (Hebrews 13:5).

Dependence is the key that frees God's hands to work for us. Without his sight, my friend was dependent upon the instruction of another, one who could see! This lesson was brought home very forcibly to me on one of the many flights I have to take as I travel to speaking engagements and seminars all over the world. I have learned to appreciate the air traffic controllers as never before. I am glad that they can see the big picture, all the dangers and obstacles on their radar screens. They are in charge, and the pilot merely carries out their instruction. But it's more than the technology. I am grateful for the very real concern that the individual controllers feel for the safety of those in their charge.

For example, as my flight made its final approach to the Salt Lake City International Airport, the controllers had done their job, and our flight, thanks to the controller's instructions and our pilot's skill, was lined perfectly with the runway. Nearer and nearer the ground came until at last we were less than 300 feet over the earth. Instead of landing, the invisible hand of gravity pressed me down into my seat cushion as the aircraft accelerated and climbed steeply upward. What had happened? The pilot informed us that the controller had noticed what the instrumentation had failed to register. The landing gear was not properly deployed. In spite of the delay while the crew rectified the problem, not a single passenger objected to the controller's warning. His warning had saved us from destruction.

But let someone suggest that God should direct our lives, that we should obey His warnings and trust His guidance so as to avoid destruction, and we become resentful, resistant, and fretful. The reason is clear. We do not feel our need or sense our danger or our need of direction. We don't come right out and say we don't need God's guidance. In fact, we usually confess our need of Him. However, our actions give lie to our confession.

It is becoming increasingly popular in Christian circles to have "a form of godliness, but denying the power thereof" (2 Timothy 3:5). For example, the phrase "What would Jesus do?" has become a popular Christian cultural icon, displayed on everything from T-shirts to toys. Pens, plaques, and posters all display the message. It has been the subject of sermons and youth groups. It sounds so good. It seems so right, and yet, it is most often humanism masquerading as Christianity. The human is asked in his great wisdom to decide how Jesus would react in any given situation of life.

Jesus Himself told us how He decided what to do or not do when He said, ". . . I seek not mine own will, but the will of the Father which hath sent me" (John 5:30). He depended constantly on the Father's direction to give Him guidance.

I have often asked people what they would have done if they had been Jesus when He received the message that His best friend, Lazarus, was dying. You and I would have run off and healed our friend, but Jesus didn't do that. He stayed right where He was and let His best friend die. You see, God had something wonderful planned for Lazarus, far more wonderful than being healed of his disease. If it had been us, rather than Jesus, we would have made a mess of those plans because we are not used to having God control our entire lives. We have not cultivated a spiritual sensitivity as Jesus had.

God says, "Cease ye from man, whose breath is in his nostrils" (Isaiah 2:22). This means cease ye from every man, including our own great prideful reasoning and intellect. It means to cease from managing ourselves, to tune into God and cultivate a daily spiritual sensitivity until it becomes a way of life.

Often an idea that seems reasonable in a theoretical setting is seen to be absurd when placed in a real-life setting. For instance, would you want to fly with a pilot who decided his actions based on what he thought the controller would tell him to do in a given situation, rather than inquiring of the controller? If you don't find this flight method very reassuring, why do we accept such practices in our religious life? Probably it is because the whole of our religious experience is unbalanced.

We humans have the idea that a balanced life consists of God and me sharing the control of my life with God pulling upward and self pulling downward. This may be balance, but it leads nowhere. Hence, we must consider whether our religion has real-life application. Does it lead us consistently upward? If not, then what we call religion is an unhappy life of constant pulling back and forth. Worse, it is a religion that permits our mental assent to truths to soothe our thinking and justify our deeds, while in reality we sit on the fence. It is the worse kind of deception for we think we are walking the path to heaven, while we stay in exactly the same place, in the same condition, and just as fit for destruction as we were before we found this thing called religion!

Remember Rob, whom we met in the preceding chapter? Rob's religious experience needed to become practical. Simple intellectual knowledge had not made him a new creature in Christ. The first step for anyone desiring to possess a life altering Christianity is to become "swift to hear" (James 1:19). The willingness to really hear is the key that opens the door to effective communication in all our relationships, and its absence is the greatest hindrance.

Harold had been raised in what he described as a "cult type" religion. Coming of age, he rejected the doctrinal stances of the group in which he was raised, except for one thing: the group's simple country lifestyle. It was still dear to his heart, his dream so to speak. At forty, Harold is typical of many Americans. He is in his second marriage and is raising three children from the two unions. He and his second wife, Jennifer, aged thirty, live in an affluent section of Connecticut just outside of New York City. Both are professionals, and together they earn a great deal of money, but their lifestyle also incurs a lot of expenses.

Now in midlife, Harold is increasingly dissatisfied. He is making it in the world but is unfulfilled. As nominal Christians, he and Jennifer have bounced around from church to church over the last few years, trying to find fulfillment. Jennifer, while lower keyed than her husband, is also searching, also dissatisfied with life. This is hardly surprising, for as a stepmother to two children from Harold's first marriage, life is often stressful. She and Harold went through a lot of difficult adjustments forming their blended family. Surely the future could only be better. Now with a small child of her own, motherhood is the longing of her heart. If only she could stay home. If only she could have more children. If only economics didn't require her to work, then perhaps she could be happy.

The property sat in a neighboring state, consisting of more than one hundred acres of fields, woods, and a lake. The house was old but in great shape, as was the barn. It was the perfect country property requiring only someone's dream to make it a reality. It was not expensive by Connecticut standards, and when Harold took a drive up to see it, he wrote an offer for it on the spot.

On the surface, it would seem this couple had compatible dreams. Surely this was a match made in heaven, but it was not to be. Very few wives would enjoy having their husband choose to purchase a property without their approval, and Jennifer hadn't even seen the land yet. Then there were Harold's great dreams for the property, which included building a new house. Jennifer, ever practical, quickly realized that she was never going to be able to stay home with all these additional expenses.

Over the months it took to close on the property, Jennifer tried to get Harold to understand her concerns, but he brushed them aside. Harold wasn't listening. He thought his wisdom was greater, his experience broader. Tension between them grew so severe that Jennifer refused to sign the purchase agreement. Now, by any measure of judgment, there was a message in all this for Harold. But if he saw it, he refused to heed its warning, tuning it all out. He felt he was entitled to his dream, and nothing was going to stop him, so he purchased the property without her. Many a wife has experienced this selective hearing. They may not have had their husband buy property without them, but there are many ways we men can be insensitive to their concerns.

The changes came slowly and gradually. Jennifer wasn't sleeping well anymore. She was sullen and dissatisfied at work. Her happiness at home was now only a bitter memory. For the first time anyone could remember, she began complaining about her husband, openly speculating on separating from him. Little things she used to overlook in love became insurmountable mountains.

Harold at last realized that his wounded wife was indeed becoming insensitive to him and decided something was wrong. He decided work must be too stressful and encouraged her to look for another job. His inability to see his own selfishness and insensitivity, his unwillingness to hear, really hear his wife, confirmed in her heart the very worst that she had thought of him, and now it was yielding its fruit in a harvest of insensitivity.

Harold has yet to have his dream. Now they pay two mortgages, one for their Connecticut home and one for Harold's dream, while Jennifer's dream of quitting work and staying home turns to ashes upon the altar of stubborn pride and willful insensitivity. How long will they last this way? It's anybody's guess. Sad, isn't it? Surely we wouldn't be so insensitive. Or are we?

When I was courting Sally, I was very sensitive to her opinions, her comments, her thoughts, and her desires. She was constantly on my mind. I would sit in class with my notebooks and write her name over and over and embellish it with hearts. However, it wasn't long after I married her that I started to tune her out, to treat her like a convenience. What happened? I communicated only when it was convenient for me or if there was some sort of crisis, and bit by bit the marriage lost its zeal, its freshness. The very qualities that made the marriage living and vibrant and a joy to experience disappeared.

In taking Christ's name, Christians are in essence claiming to be married to Him. Many of us, far too many of us, who have taken His name act just the way Harold and I acted in our marriages. We either ignore the guidance of God and pursue our goals, or we treat God as a convenience. We take time for Him when it is convenient, when we feel like it, and then rush urgently to Him if there is a crisis.

My marriage only improved when the quality of the communication Sally and I had improved, or shall I say, when I truly learned to listen to her. This principle holds true in every relationship. Effective communication always begins with listening to the other party. My relationship with God has demonstrated this principle time and time again. Listening to the voice of God is almost a lost art in today's society. So let's explore the avenues of communication between God and man.

Most people think of the Bible when they think of God communicating with the human race. Certainly the Bible conveys to our minds an understanding of God and points out the pathway to obtaining a relationship with Him. "All scripture is given by inspiration of God, and is profitable for doctrine, for reproof, for correction, for instruction in righteousness" (2 Timothy 3:16).

Yet this same book of the Bible warns us that the Scriptures may be misunderstood or misapplied. "Study to shew thyself approved unto God, a workman that needeth not to be ashamed, **rightly** dividing the word of truth" (2 Timothy 2:15, emphasis added).

Volumes have been written on Bible study, and sometimes it can be confusing. Regardless of what you have or haven't tried in the past in your study, let me encourage you to leave other books and ideas and just come to God's Word with a heartfelt desire to have God provide you with practical guidance for the upcoming day. Come to the Scriptures as a sinner in need of salvation and linger in God's presence. Be still and know that He is God (Psalms 46:10). If you do this, the Bible will become more than sacred history, more than suggestions of how to live a holy life. Often we will hear the voice of God speaking to us personally from its pages.

True religion is that religion which transforms the entire life. It is an experimental religion. It is not just theory but something we experiment with in a practical manner. Here the Bible shines forth in its brilliance. The Bible provides us an anchor, an infallible source against which we can test our understandings.

Nature still points the way to her Creator. It was within the confines of the natural world that I learned to recognize the voice of God. When the distractions of "civilized" society are eliminated, the human mind is more apt to hear the voice of God. Even though it is scarred and distorted by sin, nature still reveals the wisdom and order of our God. Amid the glory and majesty of creation, we can sense our God's mighty power and feel our own inadequacy.

However, the human mind can take even the most sublime of experiences and distort them to our own destruction. Charles Darwin traveled to a beautiful location and there, surrounded by some of the most wonderful and unusual creatures of God's creation, he felt nature was speaking to him. But the messages he felt he heard were not brought to the test of Scripture. Had he been willing to test his theories as God commands, "To the law and to the testimony: if they speak not according to this word, it is because there is no light in them" (Isaiah 8:20), then he would not have marched off into darkness and error thinking he had found new and exciting light.

God also speaks to us through His providence in our lives. In His glorious pursuit for our affections, God arranges circumstances for our benefit. This is not some arbitrary action on His part to control us, but rather, like any parent, He works to alter circumstances so that His children, you and I, can make right choices. Remember when I went to purchase the land only to have it sold out from under me at the last minute? Was God directing me? It didn't feel like it at the time, but He was and He will speak to you through the providence of life too.

There is another side to providential leadings. They are what I would call "fleeces." In Judges 6 and 7, we are told the story of Gideon whom God raised up to deliver His people. Gideon heard the Lord's instructions to him but was distrustful of his own abilities and talents, so he asked the Lord to confirm the directions given by the use of a piece of wool—a fleece.

> And Gideon said unto God, If thou wilt save Israel by mine hand, as thou hast said, Behold, I will put a fleece of wool in the floor; and if the dew be on the fleece only, and

it be dry upon all the earth beside, then shall I know that thou wilt save Israel by mine hand, as thou hast said. And it was so: for he rose up early on the morrow, and thrust the fleece together, and wringed the dew out of the fleece, a bowl full of water.

And Gideon said unto God, Let not thine anger be hot against me, and I will speak but this once: let me prove, I pray thee, but this once with a fleece; let it now be dry only upon the fleece, and upon all the ground let there be dew. And God did so that night: for it was dry upon the fleece only, and there was dew on all the ground (Judges 6:36-40).

I have used fleeces in my experience. No, I have never laid wool on the ground. Maybe it would have been better if I had in some instances, but let me share an example of one of my fleeces with you.

I was bow hunting for deer soon after I became a Christian, or perhaps I should say, thought I had become a Christian. In any case, while I was hunting I heard the Lord speaking in the quiet recesses of my mind. That still, small voice said, *Put down your bow, Jim.*

I knew this was the Lord and I knew what He wanted me to do, but I was resistant. Almost defiantly I told the Lord, "Well, if You want me to quit bow hunting, bring someone to me with a 35mm camera and telephoto lens, because I still want to go out in the woods. Oh, and Lord, they must bring it to me at half price."

I felt pretty safe after this prayer. I had given the Lord a defiant fleece, an impossible task, the faithless plea of my unsurrendered heart. I would never pray such a prayer today! But that was where I was back then.

Some time later, I got a phone call from a young man who was working in the community, selling Christian books door to door. I greeted him warmly and he asked if he could come over to see me. "Sure, come on over," I said.

He arrived shortly, with a plain, brown cardboard box in his hands. I was really curious by this point. He seemed to be in no hurry to inform me about the contents of the box. Finally, after he had comfortably seated himself, he calmly stated, "I have a story to tell you."

"Go ahead!" I blurted out.

"I was out selling books when I visited this one family, They were very interested in the complete set of *Bible Story* books that I sell, you know, the ones for children. But they really couldn't afford them. They are about the most expensive books I sell, around three hundred dollars per set. I can't express to you how badly they wanted them. I could just see it in their eyes. It wasn't just the kids, Jim. The parents loved them too. I really wanted them to be able to buy my books, but I didn't know how to help them. At this point, the father made me an offer. He said, "I have this camera. I just bought it a little bit ago. It's 35mm and has a telephoto lens. I paid over six hundred dollars for it, but I would trade you even up for the books."

My young friend paused. "Jim," he said in all seriousness, "I stood there not knowing what to say and your name came to my mind. It was like a voice said as plain as day, 'Go ahead, and accept the deal. Jim will take the camera.' So I accepted the deal. Will you take the camera?"

Words cannot tell you how low I felt. The tears flowed down my cheeks as I wrote out that check, because I knew I shouldn't have prayed that prayer, and yet the Lord understood. I got rid of the bow and I have never hunted since.

Probably the most misunderstood way in which God speaks to us is through impressions in our mind. Many people tell me, "I never hear God speak to me the way you say you hear Him speak to you!" and I always respond, "Yes you do! You just don't recognize God's still, small voice or else you have so trained yourself to ignore His promptings that you don't hear them anymore."

Have you ever noticed that people who live near a train track don't even seem to discern the trains passing, while visitors are nearly deafened by the sound? We can do the same thing with God. When we persistently ignore His promptings they just blend into the background noise until they are almost unrecognizable.

I have a friend I'll call Arnold, to protect his privacy. He came to me after a sermon and said, "Jim, you say God speaks to you, but I've never heard Him talk to me the way He talks to you."

"He speaks to you and you have heard Him," I said.

"I have?" he questioned skeptically.

"Sure you have," I encouraged him. "The last time you were in the grocery store and your eyes were drawn to the trashy gossip magazines or the ones with the scantily clad women on the front, what did the Lord say to you in your mind at that moment?"

I was fairly sure I knew the answer. Arnold may not have developed a relationship with the Lord that involved "real" communication, but I knew he claimed to be a Christian. And no one who is serious about being a Christian can behold the images of the trash, trivia, and trouble displayed by the rich and famous or look on the sensual images of the latest fashions, without the Lord prompting his thoughts, trying to protect his mind from such garbage.

"He said, 'Don't look!'" Arnold responded.

"What did you do?"

Silence.

"What did you do?" I asked again, but he wouldn't answer me. Oh, my friends, it is not that we can't hear God's voice, but that we have trained ourselves to be unresponsive to Him. I call it selective hearing. This is what causes us to think that our lives are led without His guidance.

However, not everything that pops into our heads is a prompting from the Lord. There are three areas that these ideas spring from. First, the Spirit of the Lord may prompt our thoughts. Second, our own flesh, which is made up of our passions, appetites, and desires may be the source. Last of all, we live in a world that has been tempted into rebellion against God by the devil and he is no less active in tempting us to sin than he was in any past generation. So, how can we filter the thoughts that come to us and tell them apart?

Promptings can and should be brought to the test of the Word of God. However, there are times when a prompting is neither inherently right nor wrong. An example of this was when the Lord asked me to move to the other side of the log I was cutting so that He could save my life. Morally it was not wrong to cut on either side of the log and there was no biblical principle involved against which I could test the prompting. What I did have was the beginnings of a familiarity with hearing the voice of God.

Like any friend, the more we listen to His voice, the more recognizable it will become. One rule of thumb I use to test a prompting is this: if the prompting asks me for self-denial—if it puts the needs and feelings of others before my own—I can be comfortable following it. These traits are the opposite of the sinful nature, the flesh I was born with, and they are not the character traits of Satan either.

We need to understand that the human mind, weak and failing as it is, remains the only medium through which God can communicate with any of us. Those seeking to communicate with the Sovereign of the universe should shun anything that weakens the functions of the mind. Certainly the use of mind-altering chemicals to achieve a so-called higher state of being, should make one very skeptical about supposed messages received by individuals while in such states. God is a God of reason, and He invites us to use the reasoning powers that He endowed us with in the following words, "Come now, and let us reason together, saith the Lord" (Isaiah 1:18).

Some Christians I talk to are uncomfortable with these promptings because they so closely resemble the messages received by those involved in the New Age movement.

Singer, songwriter, and composer John Denver once explained it like this: "So I listen to the voices inside me. For I know they are there just to guide me."

I have friends who are into the New Age movement, and their lifestyle closely resembles mine. They are debt free. They live in a beautiful wilderness home. They eat a healthy diet. And yes, just like me, they hear promptings in their thoughts that they choose to obey. However, they refuse to conduct their lives according to the Word of God and do not differentiate between the voices or acknowledge that these promptings could possibly be from the devil. The spirits giving them these promptings are demanding to the point on insisting which shirt they should wear. I have often challenged them to cross their spirit, to disobey. None of them will do it. They're scared of the reaction. God does not use intimidation, but binds us to Him with cords of love. Those serving the spirits of the New Age movement have no freedom, but serve the god of their thoughts. It so saddens me because they stand so close and yet so far from truth.

However much we desire God's guidance in our lives, there is a danger that we will approach God without a subdued spirit willing to obey whatever He shows us to do. If our own will is not neutralized, then there is a tendency to use our cherished ideas and goals as a standard by which to judge impressions and thoughts. When we have a thought that is in harmony with our preconceived ideas, it is not hard for us to assume that this must be a message from God.

Perhaps the largest hindrance to free and open communication with God is lack of exclusivity. God wants to go through every day with us as our constant Companion. He wants us to talk with Him throughout the day, depending upon His wisdom for guidance whether we are by ourselves, working, or visiting with friends. Perhaps you may share an inclination I have to place God on the sidelines when I have a task to do. It is almost as if I say, "All right Jesus, You sit over here. I'm going to get something accomplished."

And that is exactly what happened the day I heard my son's voice floating up the stairs. "Father, Mother wants to do a load of laundry, but the generator won't start!"

Fourteen little words were all it took to start a crisis in my life. I was at my desk studying God's Word when the call came. Surely no better time could come for a temptation than when one is studying the Bible. Or could it? Can self even strive for control when one is studying the Scriptures? It surely can! Immediately, irritated feelings rose up in my flesh because I didn't want to be interrupted. Besides, it was forty degrees BELOW zero, and I didn't want to go out to that garage and wrestle with that cold piece of iron that refused to run.

Bundling up and walking out to the generator, I looked at it and could feel the battle raging in my heart. *You're not ready to deal with this yet,* I could hear the Lord speaking in my thoughts. What does my strong German temper want to do? Have you ever kicked a cold piece of iron? The flesh doesn't care who gets hurt as long as it can vent its feelings and frustrations.

I walked back to the house and picked up a pen and paper to write the following: Independence from God—the curse of Jim Hohnberger's life!

Then I fell on my knees and prayed to the Lord until I felt subdued in my spirit. "Lord, this is our problem," I said. And it felt great to have Him carry the burden! "I don't know what's wrong with that machine, but You do, and I am going to depend on You to guide me." That felt even better! I was not going at this problem alone. Now the Lord of the universe was going to be at my side.

Returning to that troublesome machine, I felt the impression to check the points, so I checked the carburetor. After five cold minutes of fussing with the carburetor, I could find nothing wrong. The impression was still there about the points, so I checked the choke. I found nothing wrong there, so I moved on to the wiring. Still that impression didn't go away, and at last I gave in and checked the points, only to find a loose screw, which was shorting out the system.

I had gone to the Lord for help. I had even verbally placed my dependence upon Him. Then I ignored His leading. Talk about selective hearing. I had not learned the exclusivity required to make His voice, His input, supreme and all other voices—even my own "great" intellect—subordinate to Him.

Some years ago, Andrew made an old fashioned, wooden swing for Sally and me. It was a wonderful gift, and we have put it to use every day in what we like to call "swing time." At noon, Sally and I put away our work and sit together. This is Sally's time to visit and share. Sometimes our talks are about deep and heartfelt concerns. Other times it may be a simple sharing of the events of the day. It is, however, scheduled time with my queen, time to listen, to really hear her. It is time I have learned to value greatly.

A friend came up to my house right when I was supposed to have swing time with Sally. We greeted him and he explained his errand. "Are you in a hurry?" I asked.

"Well, I do have to get back to town, but I'm not in that big a rush," he responded.

"Great," I told him. "Why don't you go on into the house and grab a drink of water if you want one and help yourself to a book for a few minutes. I have an appointment with my wife."

He looked at me for a long minute and then went into the house.

My wife needed to know that she was more important to me than the unexpected visitor. This prioritizing is one of the keys to unlock a vibrant communication with God as well as with our wives. Satan works very hard to break down this communication in our marriages, for without this they begin to die. Imagine how much more Satan wants to break the communication between the soul and God! And he'll use any means he can to do it. He distracts our minds with everything from music to billboards, jamming our senses in the same manner that communist countries used to jam the Voice of America broadcasts. It takes concerted effort for us to retain a connection with God under the onslaught of noise and needless information in our modern society.

After a speaking engagement in Tennessee, my family traveled to the Nashville airport to fly on to our next appointment. Since we arrived a few minutes early, I decided to drop the family and our luggage at the departure entrance and then return the rental car, rather than mess with the luggage on the rental company shuttle. Pulling up to the departure area, we were able to park right in front of the entrance. Usually it is hard to park in these high traffic areas but today we got the best spot imaginable.

As I pulled toward the curb I felt the impression to take the keys with me, but I saw no reason to do that. After all, I could unlock the trunk with the little switch inside. But God had not given up on me and again as I got out of the car, I felt the impression to roll down the window. But it was a cold morning and I knew after unloading the luggage the warm car would feel good, so I ignored the impression. After taking the luggage inside, I went back out to return the car to the rental agency and found all the doors on the idling 1998 Chevrolet locked with the only key in the ignition. Immediately, I realized why the Lord had impressed me to take the keys and I said, "Oh Lord, I'm sorry!" My independence from God always spells T-R-O-U-B-L-E.

Now I have learned something about the airlines in all my travels—they don't wait for Jim Hohnberger if I am late. I was in big trouble because my flight was scheduled to leave in little more than an hour. I was also in trouble because you can't leave a car in this type of area more than a few minutes or the police will first ticket it, then tow it away. I ran back inside to get Andrew and had him stand by the car in case they wanted to tow it away, then I ran down to the rental car company.

The line at the car rental counter was huge. I knew my flight would leave before I ever got to the counter. Now that I was in a crisis, I was motivated to listen, really listen to God's instructions. So I prayed silently, "Lord, what should I do?"

Just go up to the counter and ask for the manager. Yes, the other people won't like it and yes, you will be embarrassed, but it will be all right.

So I walked up to the counter and asked for the manager. He told me they had no spare keys, but that they could obtain one if I got the serial number for the car. I ran back to the car only to find a policeman writing out a ticket while my son stood off to the side. He was very embarrassed about the whole situation and had not spoken up. I explained my problem to the policeman, who thankfully had mercy and allowed me a few more minutes to remove the vehicle.

Quickly I scribbled down the number and ran back to the rental agency as the minutes ticked away towards my departure time. But the manager was amazing, and the whole process took only fifteen minutes from start to finish. Soon I was headed back to the car with a new key.

As Andrew and I got back into the car I wanted to say to him, "Why did you lock the car?" I would have too, except that the Lord was speaking quite forcibly in my mind telling me to be still. "But Lord," I argued "it's obvious he did it. I didn't do it and he was the last one in the car. He probably just locked the doors out of force of habit."

Keep quiet, Jim. You'll find out down the road how it happened.

Don't say words that you will regret, the Lord replied. Well, I had only gone a little ways down the road when all the doors locked automatically. I finally realized that this 1998 Chevy had some type of timing device that locked the doors. Returning the rental car, I boarded our flight gratefully, not just because we made it in time, but also because the Lord had prevented me from falsely accusing my son. Still, there was a twinge of sadness, for I had spent the weekend preaching to others about being sensitive to the Spirit of the Lord speaking to us and I had ignored His guidance and caused the whole problem with my selective hearing.

Often the things God asks us to do don't seem to make any sense. God didn't tell me I needed to take the key because the car would lock them inside if I didn't. Instead, He depends on us to trust that He knows what He is doing and through faith in His love and wisdom to obey His instructions. I call this experimental religion for the very reason that in each of these experiences I have learned lessons and grown in my understanding, even though I didn't listen perfectly. When I see the trouble I cause by not heeding His directions, it reinforces to my mind a familiarity with His still, small voice and a future determination to quickly obey His instructions. This process of learning to listen is the essence of experimental religion. It's learning what works and what doesn't.

I was plowing snow in the driveway one day while my family was working on various housekeeping tasks. After a while, Matthew felt impressed that I was taking longer than I should to plow the drive. "Maybe I should get on the snowmobile and check on him," he said to himself. Now Matthew also loves to drive the snowmobile and because he likes it so much he was fearful that this "impression" to go check on Father was simply an excuse for him to stop work and go do something he enjoyed. Several times the impression came, and several times he reasoned it away. Then I came in all cold and snow-covered. The truck had broken down at the end of the driveway, and I had to walk back home through huge piles of snow.

Matthew then realized that the impression had come from God. But the experience wasn't a waste, because he learned from it. How do I know? Well, on another trip, I was traveling with Sally and Andrew. Matthew was home alone. I just called to check in. "How's it going?" I asked him.

"I'm learning to listen, Father." Then he told me this story. He had to take some client to see a property way up over a mountain pass. As he was leaving the house, he said that he felt a strong impression to bring a flashlight with him. That's nonsense, he told himself. After all, I'm going to be home long before nightfall. But the impression came again and recognizing the voice of God, He went back into the house and brought a flashlight with him.

"What time did you get home?" I asked him.

"Midnight."

A large spike—the kind used to connect log cabins together—had found its way into one of his truck tires. His story thrilled my heart, for as a teenager he was learning lessons of dependence and spiritual sensitivity to God that I didn't even know about when I was thirty.

Would it be any easier for us to listen and obey the Lord if He did tell us the "why" behind His instruction? My own experience would indicate, no.

When fall comes and freezing temperatures approach, one task that I must confess is not a favorite of mine must always be done—draining the water system in our guest cabin. The job isn't all that bad, but the crawl space under the cabin is dark, damp, and full of cobwebs. It's the kind of place you expect a spider or a mouse to jump out at you, and you wish you had some friend who would volunteer to do the job for you.

This cold fall day, I lifted up the trap door to the crawl space and climbed down under the cabin to drain the pipes. Needing more dexterity in my hands than I could get wearing my gloves, I set them on the ground beside me. Immediately, I felt the impression to put them in my pocket because I might forget them. Now, you can ask anyone who knows me, I have a wonderful memory. I don't forget things. So I reasoned away this impression and finished the job.

As I walked towards my house in the cold, I reached for my gloves, and you know where they were, don't you? "Oh, no! I forgot my gloves under the cabin," I wailed. I had no choice but to retrace my steps and retrieve them. In this instance, the Lord had prompted my mind, even warning me of what might happen, but the extra knowledge still did not affect my response to His instruction. I thought I knew better.

In the end, we will be faced with a choice of obedience to God's promptings. We must make that decision based on a living faith as well as knowledge. As we experiment with practical religion, allowing God increasing control in our lives, then we will find ourselves learning more and more to recognize and trust His voice. Just like me, you will have instances where you ignore His guidance and make a mess of things. But God does not abandon us when we do this, and if we are willing He can teach us valuable lessons from these errors. So experiment with God, lean more and more of your weight on Him, leap out in faith, and trust His guidance.

If you do this, you will find Him not only an infallible guide, but the best of friends to travel life's pathways with, both in this world and in the world to come.

CHAPTER 8

Our Greatest Enemy

"He must increase, but I must decrease"
(John 3:30).

William Murphy was an attractive, powerful man. Only forty, he was already an executive in a huge international corporation. For the last week however, he had been contemplating something other than mergers and contracts. He was forced to consider his own mortality. It began at dinner with a dull, persistent ache in his jaw. Nausea soon followed, washing over him in waves. He told his wife he wasn't feeling well and wanted to leave the restaurant for home. Then he collapsed on the floor.

Paramedics found him to be in a potentially fatal heart rhythm but managed to stabilize him. He regained consciousness in the emergency room and had spent the last week in a blur of tests and procedures. The diagnosis? Major heart attack. Worse yet, his cardiac catherization revealed severe blockage in another artery. Now he was scheduled for a procedure to open the blockage. This would not only prevent another heart attack but would also, he hoped, save him from coronary bypass surgery.

Thankfully, the procedure went smoothly, and he was transferred to the post-procedure unit where his wife awaited his arrival. The cardiologist soon joined them with several "before and after" pictures in his hand. Using the pictures to demonstrate, the physician explained that the 95 percent occlusion of the blood vessel had been reduced to a less than 5 percent residual blockage. As good as that was, the specialist had bad news to share also.

He said, "Your lipids—that is, your cholesterol, the fats in your blood stream—are still grossly elevated, with total readings more than twice the maximal normal. Worse for you is that the ratio of helpful to harmful fats is poor. You need to be on a cholesterol reducing medication. I've also asked dietary to come and see you due to the fact that you need to be on a strict diet until these levels drop. In about six months, we will reevaluate the diet based on the decrease seen by then. Once you have recovered, I want you in a cardiac rehabilitation program. Finally, you have absolutely smoked your last cigarette. With any luck we can prevent this blockage from reoccurring."

His pep talk over, the doctor answered a couple of questions and exited the room saying, "I'll see you tomorrow."

William waited until the cardiologist was gone, turned to his wife, said decisively, "I won't live like that!"

For a week, he had contemplated with sober thoughts the possibility of dying. Now that the specter of death had retreated under the onslaught of modern medicine, this otherwise intelligent, rational man was unwilling to take the steps necessary for his long-term survival.

Everyone thought that Bill's smoking, his diet, his high stress job, his executive lifestyle, and his family history were to blame for his condition. In the end, these risk factors were not the enemy to be guarded against. In truth, Bill's greatest enemy had already fought and conquered him. His own self-will was unwilling to sacrifice, unwilling to die. Desire was stronger than reason and appetite stronger than intellect. When William dies at an early age, his death certificate will read "death as a result of natural causes." But in truth, Bill will have been murdered, slayed by his own stubborn self-will.

When I moved to the wilderness, I was a lot like William. My spiritual life was in intensive care, in need of resuscitation. I thought I would escape from a number of enemies in the mountains—risk factors, if you will. I had thought that the worldly influences of the media were the enemy. I thought that the ministers who taught false-hood from the pulpit—the false shepherds, as the Bible calls them—were the enemy. I thought that the cares and "busy-ness" of the fast lane, work-a-day world were my enemy. I thought all these things were enemies that prevented me from living the Christian life.

And I was right. These things are enemies, and they do hinder the development of true Christianity. As much as possible they should be eliminated from our lives, so that their influence can be mini-mized.

Unfortunately, I had the idea that battling the influence of these enemies was what constituted the spiritual warfare in my life. It wasn't until I moved to the wilderness that I discovered that even in the most ideal environment I could imagine, I was still the same person who left Wisconsin. I arrived to do battle with my sins only to find those sins were nothing more than symptoms of my real problem. Let me tell you, it was a bitter pill to swallow when I realized that the real problem, the real enemy, the real risk factor I faced was ME!

I was the problem! My individual sins were just the inevitable fruit of "SELF" being in control of my life. It is here that oh so many who earnestly hope and desire to be Christians fail. God must have the whole heart that merely represents all my choices surrendered to Him. He is not interested in having some of my choices or even most of my choices, but He wants all. The key to living the Spirit-filled life is when we lay down all to the Lordship of Jesus Christ. "No man can serve two masters," Jesus said. Why? "For either he will hate one, and love the other; or else he will hold to one, and despise the other" (Matthew 6:24).

When I married Sally, I agreed to give up all my previous girlfriends. All my affections were given to her. All my former interests were relinquished. I died to my old life of singleness. Now, if I had tried to have a marriage with Sally while at the same time carrying on an affair with a previous girlfriend or friends, what would happen to my relationship with Sally? You know, don't you? We wouldn't stay married very long, would we? Suppose I excuse my behavior and declare, "But I'm still married to her. She's my wife. I'm committed to her." It's a pretty ridiculous idea even to contemplate.

Yet, this is exactly what happens with most Christians. They try to hang on to their former loves while embracing Christ. At the same time, they indignantly denounce anyone who would dare question their commitment to Christ as unloving and judgmental. After all, they are good people. They do good things. They are born again, or so they claim.

The example of the rich young ruler was included in the Bible for a reason. He was a good man and a leader. Today, many would look at him and say he was born again. However, he wanted to be married to Christ while at the same time having an affair with self. He didn't want to leave his former girlfriend for Christ. So many miss the vital lesson of this story. It was not the fact that this man had great riches that kept him from Christ, but rather that he wanted to manage his life, his riches, himself.

Seven times in Scripture, Christ referred to His cross as ours. The terms Christ offers for discipleship are very clear. "If any man will come after me, let him deny himself, and take up his cross, and follow me" (Luke 9:23). Death to self is poorly understood by both the church and by individual Christians.

It is not a one-time death but a daily dying to my will and my way. This death occurs as I willingly allow the substitution of Another's (God's) will and way no matter how crucifying this substitution is to my wishes or desires. It is when we willingly choose to give up the right to manage self that we are truly God's.

This was Christ's experience when He prayed "Not my will, but thine be done" (Luke 22:42). That Jim might gain this experience was God's goal from that very first day He launched that glorious pursuit for my life. In traditional western courtship, a woman is not won to a man until she bears his name. In the taking of his name, she pledges her willingness to surrender not just her finances, her life goals, or even her privacy, but rather that she is willing to share the most intimate areas of her being. She is going to give her very self to the one she loves.

Few who claim to be Christians desire this depth of intimacy and surrender to God. Fewer still have obtained it. Why? Because it is a process and the modern church has completely lost sight of this fact.

When you start dating someone, you do not begin at the altar. Instead, you set out to win their affections. God does the same with us. Gradually, feelings develop for the other person. At first they have a little place in your heart and you are willing to give a little of yourself for them. Then this special person becomes more important to you, and your willingness to give of yourself for them increases and continues to grow until you are merged into one flesh after marriage.

Our relationship with God is the same way. It's a gradual process leading us to a marriage that is a merging of two into one.

The worldly view of Christianity popular today confuses this process so badly that the minute one expresses any interest in Christ, they are considered to be Christians. The Bible often speaks of the "church" being married to Christ. In light of that, let's use the analogy of courtship to gain a better understanding of the process of becoming a Christian, a true Christian.

In life, the condition before marriage is singleness. We'll call it stage one. There is usually an openness to consider another state in some degree to another depending on the person. In Christianity, that state of singleness would be a life lived apart from God. The life is ruled by self only and God is not consulted. The willingness to consider Christ having a role in one's life varies with the individual.

Then in stage two, someone comes along and expresses an interest in us. Something they say or do awakens a response within and we are willing to let them into our lives, maybe just a little bit. So it is with God. He shows us His love and care and His interest creates a desire in us to let Him have a little part of our life. Many think they have become Christians at this stage, but it is only the beginning.

The interest expressed in stage two creates affection that grows into a courtship—stage three. In this stage, the desire to join lives is born. Usually, an engagement is announced. Yet the individual is still single. They still have control and can still change their mind. Nothing is written in stone, so to speak.

For the person considering Christ, the experience is very similar. God continues to woo us to Himself. The individual learns lessons of dependence and trust in God. He begins to learn to surrender the will to God. There is the desire to make God a lifelong partner. Yet self is still in control, and a fully-surrendered "marriage" has not taken place.

The fourth and last step is marriage. When both individuals are willing to forsake all others and put each other's needs above their own, the marriage takes place. They blend their wills to become one flesh. It's a daily commitment to another person.

When the human, pursued and won by the love of God, chooses willingly to fully surrender to God, it is at that point he or she becomes a Christian and is in essence "married." In this marriage self has to die, and there can be no one and nothing else that holds a higher place in the heart than God. Only after full surrender does the taking of Christ's name have any meaning.

To maintain and deepen this commitment is the new Christian's challenge; yet freedom of choice still remains. A married person can still choose to be unfaithful. The difference between changing one's mind in stage three and four is that in stage three, the commitment has never been made. God never removes the Christian's right to change his mind. He never forces us to have a relationship with Him. Instead, He constantly draws us with love.

"Jim, are you really saying that one is not a Christian until they reach stage four?" you might ask.

My answer is Yes, no one is a Christian on the basis of profession or knowledge. We are only Christians when our total dependence is placed upon God.

"But Jim," you might say, "the whole Christian world holds a different standard. I mean, all of us understand what you're saying on a theoretical level, but you've got to meet people where they are.

Perhaps this is all very well and good on an intellectual level, but is this really practical?"

It is very practical. Come with me through a typical day and see if this experience isn't what you have longed for all your life.

My day begins at 9:00 P.M. the night before. That's because if I am not in bed at 9:00, I will not get up early enough to spend the time I need with God. This time is important to me. I am passionate about it because I have found that God is passionate about me! It is a wonderful time when I can come to Him as my very best Friend and am empowered or filled with His grace for the coming day. I spend two and a half hours every morning in prayer and quiet contemplation of His Word, asking my heavenly Father to prepare me for the struggles that lie ahead about which I know nothing. Not only does He know what's coming, but He has also planned my escape. God's faithfulness to deliver me is a constant revelation to my poor dull senses of just how much He loves me.

I don't study for information or doctrine during this time. I approach God's Word as a sinner desperately needing salvation. I come to catch a glimpse of One far more Holy and powerful than I am. When one looks at a majestic mountain or of the grandeur of the Grand Canyon, the normal reaction is one of awe and wonder. Unless drugs or alcohol dull your senses, you sense the puniness, the insignificance of man. This is the vision I want to gain of God every morning, a vision that makes me realize just how weak and powerless I am. If through communion with God I can come from my time with Him with a sense of my own need, it makes me willing to take Him with me throughout my day because I know that without Him, I can do nothing.

Oh friend, these early morning hours are a lot more than just saying our prayers or reading our Bibles. It is a time to form a vital connection with God. Have you ever tried to use a toaster that wasn't plugged in? All of us have at one time or the other. When it didn't work, did you throw it out? Of course not! You plugged it in. You gave it a vital connection to the source of power. That's what we need to do with our devotions. Plug them in!

Far too many who have tried to have morning devotional time

find it just like an unplugged toaster. They say their prayers and maybe read the Bible or a devotional book, but they never find a vital, living connection with the Source of power. Linger in God's presence. Seek Him as a drowning man seeks rescue. Long not for knowledge about religion or the Bible, but rather, seek for a knowledge of God Himself; for He says, "You shall seek Me and shall find Me when you seek Me with all your heart."

Upon leaving this quiet time with God, there is always opportunity for self to rise. After breakfast this particular morning, I hurried to finish my household jobs because a friend was coming to pick me up. We have divided the household tasks in such a way that my wife doesn't have to bear the whole burden of running the household. The boys make the beds and help with both the cooking and the cleaning.

As I passed my son's room, I noticed his bed wasn't made yet and felt impressed that I should make it for him. I was in a hurry and tried to discount the impression. After all, it was his job and I wanted him to learn to be responsible. However, the impression came again and with it a reminder that I had promised God that I would do whatever He told me to do that day. So I went over and made my son's bed and headed off to complete my own chores.

Among my tasks that morning was the stove wood. Because we live way out in the wilderness, we both heat and cook with wood. I like chopping wood and don't really find it to be a chore. However, due to the very nature of the work, it is easy to let the mind wander and I found myself thinking about a friend who had a disagreement with me. The tendency in my thoughts was to see all his faults and justify my position. That same familiar voice that had communed with me that very morning again called to my heart.

Jim, you need to pray for your brother, not enter into self-justification.

"Well, Lord, what should I pray for?" You see, self had risen almost imperceptibly and now I was hesitant, unsure that I was willing.

Jim, I want you to pray that you can do something for your friend who disagrees with you. I want you to pray that you can do something that will cost you of your time, your talents, or your money.

After a moment of struggle right there at the chopping block, I chose to surrender. Self was put to death and I prayed that prayer. And wouldn't you know, within a few weeks, God answered that prayer and gave me an opportunity to do something for this man, which cost me of my time and my talents.

The thoughts are where battles are won or lost, my friends, and I had several more battles to face in my thoughts that day.

As I finished my tasks, I noticed my friend had just pulled up to the house, and I greeted him at the door. I stepped into the laundry area where my jacket hung, and what do you suppose I saw? There sat a load of wash my wife had done. It was just waiting to be hung on the line.

Jim, I want you to hang out those clothes for your wife.

"But it's not on my chore list, Lord, and my friend is waiting. Besides those are my wife's clothes."

Jim, I want you to hang those clothes out on the line for your wife. Oh and Jim, they're your clothes too.

Right then and there I had a battle to fight in my thoughts. Should I obey? If I did, what would my friend think of me, especially after I made him wait on me while I hung them out? The conflict happened so fast. It takes longer to write it out than it did for it to occur. I am happy to say I chose to surrender my thoughts and wisdom to an all-knowing God. I invited my friend in and offered him a glass of water. "I'll be just a minute," I said as I headed out the door with the laundry basket.

At the clothes line, a new battle raged. I wanted to do a quick "hurry up and get it done" job. Was I willing to do a good job and shake out all the wrinkles just as my wife would have done? The biblical principle is whatever thine hand findeth to do, do it with all thy might. My flesh wanted to rise up and control me. It would be so easy to justify self and say "she ought to be thankful I'm hanging it out at all." The Lord was with me in that seemingly insignificant time of need, encouraging me to submit and obey. Deep down, I knew from bitter personal experience that this was the only way to true happiness.

As I carefully hung each item, I became aware of eyes boring into my back. My backward glance confirmed just what I suspected. My friend was standing at the window, glass of water in hand staring at me in disbelief. It really only took a few minutes before I was able to climb in my friend's car and we were on our way.

"Jim, why were YOU hanging up your wife's laundry?" he asked me.

"First of all," I responded, "it's not my wife's laundry. It's our laundry.

Secondly, God told me to do it." Funny, I had just had that same conversation with God.

"What do you mean God told you to do it?" he asked.

"I mean, God spoke to me in my thoughts and told me to hang out the wash," I told him. My battle opened up a theme of conversation, which continued the whole morning. I had no idea that by obeying God's promptings, I would have had an opportunity to explain spiritual things to my friend, but I did. By the time we returned to my home late that morning, my friend had decided he wanted that kind of a walk with God too. You see, God knows just what is needed to reach every person. The problem is getting Jim to cooperate with Him.

Bidding my friend goodbye, I walked into the house anticipating that I would be able to spend some time in Bible study and prayer. However, as soon as I came in, I could just sense that my wife was struggling. She had been home schooling the boys. It was her day to cook the midday meal and the whole load of wash I had hung out was dry and waiting to be ironed.

Help your wife, Jim, came that old familiar voice.

"But Lord, I had planned to study." Can self be involved even in Bible study? It sure can, especially when something else comes up that crosses our plans. Each time the decision to let self die comes, it comes a little closer to home. For me, ironing is a fate worse than death. I don't like to iron clothes, not even a little bit. I do iron clothes, but I do it out of what I would call principle.

Starting on the load of clothes, I ironed a couple of shirts. Then I came to one of my wife's blouses, one with lots of little pleats on the front. They aren't easy to iron in the first place, but to iron them perfectly, you know, the way Sally would iron them, required the sustaining power of God. By the time I finished the blouse, Sally left her meal preparations to come over to look at it. It passed her inspection! I couldn't believe it! Praise God! I felt triumphant, and for the first time I found some joy in ironing the clothes.

I was mostly done with the load of ironing when Sally called us to eat. It was a lovely meal. She made all my favorites: peas, corn, wild rice, and homemade biscuits. Little did I know that my next battle with self was just moments away. As we sat down to eat, I noticed that there was a small container of home-canned tomatoes on the table. Now, that may not seem important to you, but I LOVE home-canned tomatoes. I like to pour them over things like rice or even corn, but there was a problem, and I knew it at first glance. There was only enough for one serving in the jar, and to my side sat my eldest son, who likes them every bit as much as I do, if not more.

I bowed my head to say the prayer, but even as I prayed my flesh screamed out to me. *Grab them quick! Get them before Matthew does. You deserve them. After all, you paid for them.* Have you ever heard your flesh speak that way to you?

I don't even need to tell you what the Lord told me to do, do I? And again I faced a choice. So I sat there and watched Matthew eat those tomatoes, and you know something? I survived. Isn't that amazing? To listen to the voice of my flesh and the longing of my appetite, you would have thought that my life itself depended on those tomatoes.

The meal over, my sons went to work on the dishes. Sally took over the drudgery of the ironing, and I found myself with some free time, sitting down in the recliner with my Bible. A slight noise announced the fall of something plastic, and sure enough the cap to the spray starch had fallen at Sally's feet. *Pick that cap up for your wife, Jim,* the familiar voice of my constant Companion whispered. At first I wanted to argue and say, "It's right there at her feet. All she has to do is pick it up. I am reclined and comfortable. Why do I have to get it?" Thankfully, the Lord doesn't enter into such controversies with us. He simply lays out the path of duty and it is up to us to follow without excuse or complaint.

I set the Bible aside and returned the recliner to its upright position. I walked over and picked up the cap then set it on the ironing board and returned to my chair. As I sat down I met Sally's loving gaze. That look told me everything. I knew she understood the self-denial it required for me to get up out of that chair. The knowledge of her sympathy and the fact that my simple kindness had deepened her love for me more than repaid my effort.

Towards the end of the evening, my son came to me. I could see something had deeply moved him, but I had no idea what it was. He hesitated and then spoke. "I saw you make my bed this morning," he began. "All day long I waited for you to take credit for it, but you never did. Can we talk about the Christian walk, the one you're having."

So now you have met my worst enemy—ME! We each have an enemy to do battle with. What are you going to choose to do with your enemy—yourself? It is easy to laugh over the things we do to ourselves, but in the final analysis it is no laughing matter. In allowing self to remain and rule in our lives, we are killing ourselves just as surely as one who commits suicide.

I have spent much of my own life seeking MY way and looking to make ME happy. Let me tell you, it was a miserable existence! When we choose not to surrender self, not to allow that old carnal nature to die, then it is that all the conflict and discontent of life rises within us, not only ruining our enjoyment but also doing the same to all about us.

Within us lies the ability to choose whatever level of existence we want. The freedom to choose, the ability to exercise our will, is the greatest gift with which God has endowed the human race. Properly used, the human power of choice connects us to the God of the universe, and through His power and direction we will become a blessing to the world. Improperly used, the same power of choice will guide the human into actions that make the whole world shudder. Look back at history, examine the dictators, those whose very names have become synonymous with evil and realize that in every case, it all began with a little seemingly insignificant choice to have their own way.

In the words of James Russell Lowell:

Once to every man and nation
Comes the moment to decide,
In the strife of truth with falsehood,
For the good or evil side; . . .
And the choice goes by forever
'Twixt that darkness and that light.

CHAPTER 9

Do You Really Believe?

"Lord, I believe; help thou mine unbelief"(Mark 9:24).

One of the blessings of living in the wilderness is water of a wonderful quality. However, I felt I could make life easier by installing a gravity-flow water system. This type of system will not work on every property, but if the elevations are correct, there is nothing better in a wilderness setting. It requires no power and there are no parts to break down.

Our property is one of those fortunate ones with a spring sitting about eighteen feet uphill and two thousand feet from our home. To have gravity-flow water, all we had to do was have a back-hoe come and dig a deep trench below the frost line and lay over two thousand feet of pipe. Unfortunately, after laying the two-inch pipe, I found that I needed to go to town for some pipe fittings. An early morning trip to town would give me time to buy the fittings and install them before the back-hoe operator arrived at 9:00 A.M. to start back filling the trenches.

Rising at my normal time of 4:30 A.M., I felt the pressure of the three-hour round trip to town, and in my mind the inclination was to rush through my personal time with the Lord, so I could get to town. "You understand Lord, I usually spend time with You, but this morning I have things to do."

Thankfully, the Lord impressed my mind with this thought, *Jim, you need to spend time with Me and make sure you have a vital connection, rather than a casual connection. Stay with Me until your flesh is subdued.*

Surrendering my plan to the Lord, I stayed and had my personal time with Him. I left the house contemplating my subject of worship that morning, which was John 15:5: "I am the vine, ye are the branches." I was thinking about the close and vital connection the branches have with the vine as I drove toward town along the deserted North Fork Road.

Suddenly, a big mule deer leaped out of the ditch on the side of the road in front of me. There wasn't even time to hit the brakes before I hit him broadside at fifty miles an hour. There was a sickening thud of the impact accompanied by the sound of breaking glass and plastic. The hood accordioned and the grill gave way. Steam rose from the radiator as jagged fragments of the grill punctured its surface. The fan's clickety-clack joined the hiss of the radiator to make a very forlorn sound. The radiator had been pushed all the way back to the engine block. Leaving a small trail of broken parts, I came to stop at the side of the road.

The last thing I felt like doing at this point was abiding in the Vine. Yet as I sat there still holding on to the wheel, I could hear that soft, still voice, which never ceases to call for our attention. *Jim, you need Me right now. Do you believe I am still with you right now and can work out this problem for you?*

"Lord, it doesn't feel like it. I mean, my plans to obtain the parts seem as good as lost. The back-hoe man is coming and I'm not going to be there to meet him. My truck is destroyed. The fan is going clickity-clack. The steam is rising. Not only will I not be home at 9 A.M., I will be lucky to make it home tonight. No, Lord, it doesn't feel like You're with me right now." I wanted to get out and examine the damage, but as usual, God had other plans for me.

Jim, do you remember that breakfast your wife packed for you?

"You have got to be kidding! My truck is smashed and you want me to sit here and eat!"

Jim, if you don't eat now, you won't have time later. Your blood sugar will drop. You'll get weak and irritable. You need to get out the granola and eat it slowly and quietly.

"Eat it slowly?! Why Lord, I can't even do that at home, let alone here in my smashed truck!"

Just trust Me, Jim.

"But, Lord."

Chew slowly, Jim.

So I sat there and ate slowly, or at least I tried to. At the end of twenty minutes, I was done with the granola. I was wondering if an angel was going to appear, but none showed up. *Jim, you know that apple your wife packed for you?*

"Lord," I exclaimed, "the apple too?"

So I sat there, slowly eating my apple. As I finished the apple I saw a U.S. forest service truck coming up the road from the other direction. As the truck rolled to a stop, I gratefully realized that I knew the driver.

"Well," he said as he pulled up to my window, "you're in quite a fix here."

"I sure am," I agreed.

"Listen," he responded. "I have a dispatcher radio phone here in the truck. Do you want me to call a wrecker for you?"

"Yes, please."

After he placed the call, he went on his way, and I was left to contemplate the fact that someone else had come along the deserted road and that he had a radio phone in the truck. This was long before the days of common cellular phones, and radio phones were rare.

I felt impressed that I should get out of the truck and pick up all the glass and parts I had scattered over the road. That way, no one else would be inconvenienced by my trial. As I picked up the last of the parts, the wrecker from town came up and proceeded to hook up my truck.

"Where do you want me to take it?" The driver asked.

I remembered that I had sold some property to a nice man who owned a body shop, so I gave the driver his name. As I rode along in the cab of the wrecker, I realized I was going to have to get some type of rental car and again the temptation was to worry over the details. As strange as it might sound for a former insurance agent, I had no rental insurance, and I felt irritation rising in my heart. This was going to cost me money and lots of it!

"What happened, Jim?" asked the body shop owner who recognized me as I walked in the door.

"I hit a deer," I responded.

"Well, I must say you did a good job of it," he said while surveying the damage with an experienced eye. Looking up at me, he asked, "How are you going to get around?"

"I don't know," I said.

"Well I do," he responded. "This car rental place was just in here the other day and they gave me a bunch of coupons for free rentals. They're yours!"

"Thank You, Lord," was all I could breathe to myself. Just then the tow truck driver stuck his head in the office and offered me a ride to the car rental agency, which I gladly accepted. I got a car and the parts, and I even made it back home in time to get the job done.

At some point, everyone who claims to believe in the Lord must confront himself with the question, "Do I really believe?" Did I really believe that I was the branch abiding in the Vine that morning? The branch does not spend any time worrying over whether the vine is going to take care of its needs. It simply concentrates on growing. None of my worries that morning accomplished anything. The Lord worked out all the details, and He did it without any help from me.

Christ spoke to the people of His day about worthless worries in these words: "Therefore take no thought, saying, What shall we eat? or, What shall we drink? or, Wherewithal shall we be clothed? . . . for your heavenly Father knoweth that ye have need of all these things. But seek ye first the kingdom of God, and his righteousness; and all these things shall be added unto you" (Matthew 6:31-33).

Do we really believe? I wonder.

As I shared earlier, there are many bears in our area. I rejected the idea of arming myself for protection. Instead, I decided to depend upon the Lord to defend me and warn me when there was danger. Many people viewed this attitude of dependence upon God as presumption, and even I knew that some time, some place this plan of mine was going to be put to the test. Then and only then would I have the opportunity to confirm whether I really believed in my God.

The opportunity came, but not exactly in the way or at the time I expected it to. I wish I could say to the Lord, "At 11:00 tomorrow morning, I will be ready to be tested on patience." But it doesn't work that way. We must always be ready to give an answer for the faith that lies within us.

One day the ravens were carrying on in the woods. This usually means some type of animal has died. My boys were concerned that one of the deer we pet and feed treats by hand to might have died, so they asked if they could go exploring to find out. I not only gave them permission to go but agreed to go along too. Now, young boys do not always want to move at the same pace as their father, and I let them move on ahead toward where the ravens were crying. The trail ahead split into two different paths paralleling each other. The boys took one and I unknowingly took the other.

The idea that there might be a grizzly bear on the carcass never occurred to me. It had however, occurred to a bear. Thankfully, my two boys were quite young and excited. They made sufficient noise that the bear heard them coming and decided to leave with all possible haste, right down the trail I was walking. The bear and I met face to face at close range. The bear reared up on it haunches, growling and snarling. Grizzlies seem to hold the opinion that if you aren't looking for trouble, you should keep your distance, and if you want trouble, they will be only too happy to oblige.

I had always known that some day this would happen. Secretly, I wondered how I would react in that moment. Would I turn tail and run or drop to the fetal position and cover my head as all the experts on bear attack instruct people to do? Maybe I would try and climb a tree or fall to my knees in desperation. None of these thoughts came to mind.

As I stood eye to eye with that most-feared beast of the wilderness, I sensed not fear but Someone stronger standing by my side. In almost a casual gesture, I reached out and broke off a small twig from the branch in front of me and said, "Lord, she's all Yours!"

Friends find it hard to believe that my pulse wasn't racing wildly, but it's true. There was no panicked rush of adrenaline or sweat on my brow, just a quiet assurance that I was in the hand of my constant Friend and Companion. I knew that the Sovereign of the universe was my Shield and Protector.

One of my favorite promises in all the Scriptures is, "I will never leave thee, nor forsake thee. So that we may **boldly** say, The Lord is my **helper, and I will not fear**" (Hebrews 13:5-6, emphasis supplied).

Still gazing at the bear—which seemed to have materialized out of nowhere—I worried that my boys might come down the path looking for me. I wanted to yell and warn them to stay where they were. However, this would be inviting disaster for me. Yell at a black bear, and it will usually run. Yell at a grizzly, and it will charge. My choice was easy—as a parent I had to protect my boys.

"Boys! Stay where you are!" I shouted. True to form, the grizzly dropped down to all fours and started to charge me when suddenly she wheeled about to look behind her. My boys have been trained from the time they were little to come immediately when called. So, when I called out "Boys," they didn't even wait to hear the rest, they simply came running.

It was their voices and the noise of breaking twigs and branches as they moved toward us that dissuaded the bear, from charging. Soon my boys appeared on the other side of the bear, who was by this time both furious and desperate to escape these strange creatures who did not play by the usual rules. Taking a wide detour around me some thirty feet off into the woods, the bear returned to the trail behind me all the while growling and sputtering, leaving us with no doubt about her feelings toward us. Then she turned and ran down the path away from us.

Talk to anyone who lives in bear country. We did everything wrong you can do in a bear encounter, still we had been protected due to the benevolence of a living God, Who not only controls all the creatures of this world but also walks by our side.

Not that long ago I had to fly to Akron, Ohio. From my local airport in Kalispell, Montana, there is no direct flight. All flights are routed through the airline hub at Salt Lake City. My flight to Salt Lake City was uneventful, and as I boarded the flight for Cincinnati, Ohio and found my assigned seat, I had no idea things were about to go as wrong as they possibly could.

The captain announced there was a mechanical problem and that our flight would be delayed. Immediately I prayed, "Lord, You know I have a connecting flight to Akron that I have to be on. Please help these men to resolve this problem quickly."

Instantly, I sensed this was going to be a trial. I had only forty-five minutes between my arrival in Cincinnati and my departure for Akron. I was scheduled to speak that evening and if I missed this connecting flight, all those people would be kept waiting. So I prayed, "Lord, You know the need of those people. Don't let the devil triumph. I know You can get this plane off with enough time to spare. Please Lord, help these men get this plane off with time to spare!"

Twenty minutes passed, then thirty, then forty minutes, and the captain announced that we would be taking off in five minutes. "Lord, forty-five minutes. I'll miss my flight. It will be departing as I arrive. There is no time to spare, not even one minute." As I poured my heart out to the Lord, He prompted my mind with these thoughts:

Jim, do you believe I am with you?

"Well—yes—I preach that."

Do you believe, Jim? Do you really believe that I can hold that flight for you?

"Yeesss," I said with a little trepidation "I believe You can."

Do you believe that I will?

Now that's a much deeper question, isn't it? "Yes, I do."

Will you do all you can in order to make that flight?

"Yes, Lord."

Then I will hold that flight for you.

So I asked a passing flight attendant, "Can you have the pilot call ahead and hold that plane for me?"

"Sir," she said gently, "we have more than four hundred people on this plane. We can't be doing that for four hundred passengers."

"But," I explained, "it's not that Grandma and Grandpa are waiting for me at the airport. There is a whole auditorium full of people, and I'm the speaker and if I'm not there,—"

"I'm sorry, Sir."

I thought maybe she was just hard to get along with or I had approached the subject wrongly, so I tried another flight attendant and got exactly the same response. So I changed tactics and asked something that would seem to be very selfish, but I wasn't asking it for myself, but rather on behalf of the poor people who would be waiting for me in that auditorium.

"Ma'am, could I be the first person out that door when we come to the terminal?"

She looked at me as if to say, "My, but you're rather self-centered, aren't you?" After I shared my dilemma with her, she was very obliging. "Yes, as soon as the plane comes to a halt, come by this door, and I'll stand here with you. When that door opens, GO!"

"Great," I said to myself, "God is with me, and the airline people are cooperating. God is going to hold that plane." Cincinnati is a huge airport with many terminal buildings and an endless maze of gates. I asked the flight attendant who was helping me exactly where I had to go in the giant complex to catch my flight. It was three terminals away! So I took my sweater off and put it over my arm. I knew this was going to be a rather hot experience. With the sweater and the briefcase, I was at the door when it opened.

Several years ago there was a commercial showing a football player running through the airport, leaping over baggage, and dodging other passengers. Remember that one? Well that was me! I was jumping and dodging and running. I was perspiring when I arrived at my gate and said, "Where's the flight?"

There was nobody there except the attendant who said, "Sir, it left five minutes ago."

"But God said He was going to hold it for me!" I blurted out.

She looked at me. I mean, she really looked at me. I wish you could have seen her expression. "Sir?" she said, questioningly.

"Ma'am, you have to call the pilot and bring that plane back in, because I have to be on that flight. God assured me that flight would be held." I could see the plane as it was being taxied out. "Can't you get a truck and put me up on a ladder? I mean there it is! You have to get me on it!" But she wouldn't do it.

She looked at me like, what in the world has gotten into this guy! I knew, in my mind, that God was the God of all flesh, and that there was nothing too hard for Him. I had believed that! Did I really hear God speak to me? Was He really the God of all flesh as the Bible says? Did He really care about getting me to that appointment? I walked away from the attendant's podium and sat down in one of the chairs in the departure area, bowed my head and prayed, "But Lord you said—"

*The Lord said to me, Jim do you **really** believe that I am the God of all flesh? Do you really believe that I can bring that plane in even now if I choose to?*

I said, "Lord, I . . . I don't know. I'm not sure. I don't know, I thought I did. I did everything I could, just as You asked me to. I believed Lord. I truly believed, but the evidence is before my eyes. . . . Yes, I believe Lord, but help thou my unbelief."

As I was sitting there in that chair wrestling and struggling to come to terms with what had just happened, the attendant tapped me on the shoulder. She said, "Sir." I looked up at her, and she continued, "I don't understand it, but the plane is coming back to the gate."

"Praise God!" I said leaping to my feet. "What happened?"

"I don't know," she said. "I don't know."

"You have to find out!" I implored her.

"I will, I will. I want to know too!"

She got on her phone and called down there and then called me over to explain. It seemed that the man who was directing the plane, you know, the one who is always standing there with the cone-shaped flashlights, noticed that the front tire was frayed, and he ordered it back in for a tire change. This was what was going on while I sat in my chair with my head bowed and God was asking me, *Do you really believe, Jim?*

I hope to meet that attendant someday, because I have to ask her some questions. I was so excited about getting on that flight that I didn't say anything at the time, but I wanted to ask her, "Do you believe in my God?" I want to ask her because I could tell from the look in her eyes, that she thought I was just kind of "different." Someday I want to ask her, but I may never have the opportunity. So I want to ask you. Do you really believe in my God?

Friends, God delivered me from the grizzly bear. He provided everything I needed when my truck was destroyed. He brought the airplane back in for me. Do you believe He is just that personal of a God for you? Do you think He can deliver you from all of your problems? Do you really believe that God has the solution for every difficulty or perplexity you may face?

No, you don't! And that is why we have problems in our homes with our children, with our spouses, and in our churches. Why don't we see that hand of God in our lives like this? Where is the problem? Do you think the problem lies with God? The problem is us! We are so busy finding our own solutions in our own wisdom that we never go to the God of the whole universe who has the solution. We don't go to the Lord and say, "Lord, I need You. Please take me step by step out of my troubles."

"Why," I asked the Lord, "couldn't You have had the plane there at the gate? I would have believed."

Because it is in the darkest hour that I shine the most, Jim. Did you have a role to play? Yes, but remember Zechariah 4:6 says, 'Not by might, nor by power, but by my spirit, saith the Lord of hosts.' Jim, it is so you will understand that none of your talking to the flight attendants, none of your fantastic running through the airport, none of your trying to convince the attendant to put you up in a ladder did you any good. I had you do them to see if you would obey and cooperate with Me, but there's no power in anything you can do. It's all in Me.

God often allows us to come to the darkest hour so that He may deliver us, to remind us that He is the great God of the universe. When we seek God continually in all things, then we can experience His keeping. The Christian life is made up not only of surrender to His leading, but also a receiving of His power. ". . . As many as received him, to them gave he power to become the sons of God" (John 1:12).

God wants to give His children power to deliver them from all their difficulties, trials, and perplexities. Isaiah 58:11 says, "The Lord shall guide thee continually." Don't you want that? God wants to manage your life, your affairs. Will you agree to be led? Then you will have a personal experience with God. You will have a story to tell. It may not be about an airplane, but I guarantee that you will have a story to tell of God delivering you from your troubles. Then you can tell others how God has delivered you that they may be believers too. That is why God allows me to have these experiences, so that others may believe and not just myself.

So, let me ask you again, "Do you really believe in my God?"

CHAPTER 10

God
All in All

"Not that we are sufficient of ourselves to think anything as of ourselves; but our sufficiency is of God" (2 Corinthians 3:5).

"Jim, would you come to the realtors' meeting next month and share the secrets to your success with the other agents?" the owner of the real estate agency asked.

"I'd be delighted to," I responded and went happily on my way. I was flattered. After all, when I started my wilderness real estate practice, a number of these same professional realtors had expressed the opinion that I would starve up in the mountains. Now I was the number one realtor in their ranks, thanks partly to the fact that nobody else worked my valley. That meant I got all the listings and made all the sales. I had been in sales all my life and I felt I understood a thing or two about the relationship between buyers and sellers. Certainly I could share the methods and techniques that had helped to make my practice prosperous.

All was well until my quiet time with the Lord the next morning. The Lord asked me a question to which I had no ready answer.

Jim, are you going to tell those realtors the REAL reason for your success? Or are you simply going to share with them the part that your humanity has played in helping you succeed?

"But, Lord," I protested, wishing to avoid the trend of our conversation, "they don't want to know You—the Man behind my methods. They are just interested in my techniques."

I knew that the businessmen and women were not expecting any type of spiritual emphasis and a battle raged in my mind. What would happen if I got up and told the real secret of my success? I could picture them asking me to leave right in the middle of my speech. At the very least, even if they didn't throw me out, I knew they wouldn't understand where I was coming from and it was likely that all my fellow realtors would reject me and turn from me.

"No, Lord. I just can't do that!" But the impression wouldn't go away. I had to deal with it and at last I told the Lord that I would tell them the real secret to my success.

The day arrived, and as I stood in the podium and looked out on those individuals gathered to hear my secrets, I trembled. I wondered how my message would be received. I sensed my dependence had to be upon God.

This was not the first time in my life that I found myself battling a mixture of fear and dependence on God in my heart. Before we go on, let me share this story.

The steady intake of air sounded strangely muted under the waters of the quarry. Sally, my dive partner, looked trim and professional in spite of her missing buoyancy compensator. It was a look that belied our limited experience. Our compensators, while ordered, had not arrived. Newly certified, we had returned to the quarry to practice our skills. For that day's dive, we were wearing old-style life vests with a mouthpiece through which we could add air as needed. Both of us wore weight belts, fins, masks, and tanks which were, of course, equipped with regulators containing gauges and mouthpieces.

Sally and I had performed our open water certification dives at this same quarry. A lot of time had been spent in class learning how to regulate buoyancy. The human body when the lungs are filled with air is naturally buoyant. This means that, when immersed underwater, it will tend to rise towards the surface. For a diver to remain under the water, he must use one of two methods. The first is propulsion. The diver uses his own efforts to exert the force necessary to keep his body under the surface in exactly the same way the child in a swimming pool does when they duck under the water to retrieve an object from the bottom of the pool.

Scuba divers whose very objective is to spend time under the surface of the water have no desire to spend all their time and effort in maintaining a certain depth. Hence, they favor the other option— they wear weights to overwhelm their natural buoyancy, allowing them to slip beneath the surface with ease. However, not just any old amount of weight will do. The diver works hard to strike a balance between the weight's tendency to pull one down and the natural buoyancy's wish to pull them up. Buoyancy compensators allow the diver to increase or decrease their buoyancy by adding air as needed to the vest-like device. Theoretically, the old-style, air-filled life vests that Sally and I wore worked the same way.

I had studied the principles of diving and knew the physics involved. Reaching the bottom of the quarry at the fifty-foot level, I found I was a little too negatively buoyant and was bouncing off the bottom, stirring up clouds of silt that obscured my vision and made the dive less enjoyable.

Remember, I knew the principles that regulated diving. Those principles told me that if I added some air to my vest, I would stay off the bottom. So I dropped the regulator, took the mouthpiece to the vest, and blew and blew. But for some reason, I was unable to get much air into the vest.

As I later learned, the reason was the depth. The deeper you go under the water, the more pressure is exerted on every square inch of your body. Hence, I couldn't apply enough force from my lungs to overcome the pressure surrounding the life vest, so no air went into the vest. Another complication is that when you blow your air out at that depth with the surrounding pressure, you really blow your air out! Therefore, when I gave up on the vest and reached for my regulator, I was in real need of another breath.

But I couldn't find my regulator. As an amateur, I didn't fully realize that it had drifted behind me. Another amateur mistake had been to place my tank too high, preventing me from being able to look behind myself and find it. I was ready to panic.

I had only a few choices. I could take off my gear and find my regulator, but I was not very adept at such maneuvers. I could go off and look for Sally or any other diver, although no one was in clear view at the moment. I knew that any diver—even one who had never seen me before—would share their air with me. Last of all, I could make a free ascent up to where I knew there was air. I opted to make a free ascent.

This option had another problem. A diver can rise no faster than his bubbles if he is to prevent the "bends," a very painful, sometimes life-threatening condition where there is too much nitrogen in the blood. I had no air left in my lungs to blow out any bubbles, so I picked a pace that seemed about right and began to plan for the "what if's."

What if I couldn't make it to the surface before I passed out from lack of air? This was a real possibility! My body was screaming for oxygen at this point. I placed one hand on the release clip for my belt and the other on the control for my CO_2 cartridge. My vest was equipped with the cartridge to inflate it when it was serving its normal purpose of being a life vest. I knew that inflating it fully would draw me to the surface and even if unconscious it would hold me up out of the water. Dropping the weight belt would allow the vest to pop me to the surface even faster, but I wasn't going to risk the bends unless I absolutely had to.

About half way up, it happened! Involuntarily, I tried to breathe and there was only water. I know what a drowning person must feel. I pulled with both hands and as the vest inflated and the belt dropped away, I popped up to the surface coughing, sputtering, and gagging. Floating on the surface, I was thankful for the sea of air that surrounded me. I had been in a hostile environment, one in which man was never intended to live. While in that inhospitable location, my full dependence was upon my breathing apparatus. When I lost hold of my breathing apparatus, the environment in which I found myself began a coldly unmerciful attempt to destroy me.

So it is with you, my friends. All of us live in a world filled with sin, an environment God never intended us to live in. So we must place our full dependence upon God—our breathing apparatus, so to speak. When we lose sight of our dependence, we find ourselves adrift in the sea of sin, an ocean just as full of peril as being trapped in the deepest sea.

There is a problem. You know and I know it from experience. Our whole existence seems almost by design to hinder this type of moment-by-moment dependence upon God. Life is very bold! All sorts of thoughts and feelings leap out and demand our attention. The seductive beauty of the advertisers' models captivate our interest. The decibels and the hypnotic beat of modern music insist that we listen. The pull of our own flesh, its demands and its wishes come at us with almost overwhelming intensity. Unless we remain in a state of dependence, it is little wonder we find ourselves letting go of God.

Most of us have an inbred desire for friend-to-friend communication with God. But, in reality, no matter what we desire, we usually end up communicating with ourselves. We mull over thoughts and fret about what might happen in the future. This proclivity to analyze our situation often results in our failing to engage in any sort of meaningful dependence upon God. Because we have thought it out and in so doing drawn our own conclusions, we are led all too frequently to ignore the quiet voice of God speaking through our conscience. An awful lot of us are like Joyce in the following story.

"Joyce, how are you?" came Sarah's voice in the post office.

"Oh," said Joyce looking up. "Hi, Sarah. To tell you the truth, I am really dragging."

The two women were friends, members of the same church, but always opposites. Joyce had a career and was a single mother to her children due to several failed marriages. Sarah was a stay-at-home mom in a happy marriage. As Joyce shared her hectic life, Sarah looked with sympathy at her hassled friend. It was clear that life was running Joyce, rather than Joyce running her life. Sarah had been there and knew that it was only when she developed her schedule was she able to control the demands of her life. She gently suggested that perhaps Joyce would find life a little calmer if she adopted a schedule.

Joyce knew Sarah was rigidly scheduled, and while this might be all right for Sarah's family, she resented the implication that her life was out of control. Assuming the attitude of a sage, worldly-wise woman, she spoke down to Sarah, as if speaking to a child with whom her patience was wearing thin.

"You just don't understand what it is like to be a single mother." Joyce said testily, using an oft-repeated line that was becoming habit for her. "Besides, I have a schedule. It's just more spontaneous than yours is."

With this, she walked away and Sarah sadly watched her go. While somewhat amused by the oxymoron of a "spontaneous schedule," she was mostly hurt by her friend's attitude.

"If only she had been willing to listen." she explained later. "I could have helped her, but she just wasn't willing." Joyce walked away from what might have been, spurning the very hands that had been lifted to remove her burden.

Why do I relate such a story? Because you and I are a lot like Joyce. We have thought out our situations, planned them out, become so convinced that we have no other option, that when Jesus suggests another course of action to us, we are often like Joyce. We leave Him sad, hurt, and longing to lift our burdens, but unable to help us because we are unwilling.

The biblical history of God's people is, to a greater or lesser degree, played out in each of our lives. The Jewish nation refused God's guidance and killed the messengers He sent them. We refuse His leadership and then we blame those who bring us a message of rebuke. How often might the words Christ spoke of Jerusalem be applied to us? "Thou that killest the prophets, and stonest them which are sent unto thee, how often would I have gathered thy children together, even as a hen gathereth her chickens under her wings, and ye would not! Behold, your house is left unto you desolate" (Matthew 23:37-38).

As I travel the globe, I stay in an awful lot of desolate houses—

the homes of people who sincerely believe they are Christians. I meet so many people who are prisoners of their thoughts. Often they are living in the past, consumed by yesterday's wrongs. They spend their days in self-justification.

These individuals are often the very first to admit they made mistakes but seem blind to the fact that they have learned nothing from them. Their past errors resulted from dependence upon themselves and the pattern continues to this day, as their thoughts continue to rule in their lives.

A woman who came up to me vividly demonstrated this. I had been holding a series of meetings and I watched her mournful figure trudge up the aisle. Her eyes downcast, she seemed burdened with the weight of the world. "Brother Hohnberger," she began, "I want to talk to you about my husband." She appeared to be alone. I hadn't noticed any men nearby that appeared to be connected with her. Already I was feeling impressed that whatever the woman's problems were, her husband was not the source of them.

"May I ask you a question?" I inquired of her. She nodded, although she seemed disconcerted by this unexpected query. "Ma'am, how long have you been thinking evil thoughts about your husband?" She just stared at me, so I continued. "I can see it all over your face. I bet you have never had freedom in your thoughts toward your husband. Have you?"

"No," she admitted. She had not.

"Now, you want me to talk to you about your husband. He is not even here. If you want to talk about your husband, bring him here, but I can't do it without him. I can, however, tell you how you may have freedom in your thoughts, how you can have a right attitude towards him for the first time in your married life. If you want to talk to me about that, I'll be glad to help you."

This woman had dwelt on negative thoughts until it had affected her whole facial expression. She looked sour and unhappy because she was sour and unhappy. She wanted to speak of her husband's faults and how to get him to reform. The very best way to get a spouse interested in reformation is for you to have a reformation in your life.

Why would her husband want anything to do with this woman's religion when she was obviously miserable?

If the thoughts are not under the control of Christ, we deceive ourselves if we think we are Christians. Our thoughts and our feelings make up the character we possess and therefore it is essential that Christ control them. If we are willing to submit our thoughts to Him, then they will no longer control us. But it is more than just a surrendering of our thoughts. More specifically, it is a decided willingness to yield to our Lord's judgment when He calls for us to surrender ANY thought to Him.

I used to think that such a situation would make me miserable, would reduce me down to the level of a robot. Nevertheless, when I tried it, I found there is a special freedom that comes with constant dependence. Things suddenly seem to work out for you in a manner that you could have never dreamed and you find joy in life precisely because someone else was in control. Let me illustrate.

After a weekend speaking engagement, we found ourselves only a day's drive from Sally's mother. Realizing this ahead of time, we had planned our itinerary to include a rental car and some time to drive down and visit her. Most of the time, airport rentals are straightforward with a certain rate and unlimited mileage. This particular location didn't offer unlimited mileage, and I had negotiated a rate including the type of mileage I needed with the international reservations 800-number.

Arriving at the rental counter, I found three other customers in front of me. The poor woman at the counter appeared to be new on the job and struggled through the computer system while the customers complained about the delays. At last the others had been cared for and it was my turn. I was the last customer, no one was behind me and I could just sense she was tired. Other customers had been rude and when she pulled up my reservation everything about it was wrong!

Jim, apologize to this woman for being a thorn in her side, the Lord impressed my thoughts.

"Apologize? Lord, for what? I haven't done anything to her that's been improper." This is the tendency towards self-justification that so often we allow to push God aside as we try to run our own lives. I could rationalize my feelings. I was tired too. I had a long drive in front of me and what my flesh wanted was for this woman to get herself together and treat me right.

Jim, I want you to apologize, not because of what you have done but for the sake of this woman.

I still wasn't fully convinced but I turned to the woman and said, "I'm sorry to be a thorn in your side."

She looked at me in shock for a moment, then responded, "Sir, I . . . er . . . I mean, you're not a thorn in my side. It has just been one of those days."

"Do you think we can work this problem out?" I asked gently.

"Sir, I'm sure we can!"

And she did, although it required a call to the international reservations number and two calls to her boss at home on Sunday. I left an hour later with the right car and the right rate. "I know it's been a rough day, but hang on to Jesus," I said as I left the counter. "He has the strength to get you through."

I'll never forget her response. She smiled an endearing smile and said, "Thank you so much for being so understanding!"

It required an hour of time that I wanted to spend driving to my destination, but in choosing self-denial, I left that airport on top of the world! I knew that God had used me to touch another person's heart and encourage them!

I don't naturally possess the wisdom to know what to say to diffuse a hard situation like that. But I'm learning that if I will keep my dependence upon God, lives can be touched. And in the process, I am transformed and awed by the wisdom and mercy of my Father who cared so much for this woman and her hard day that He wanted to use me to speak words of sympathy to her.

Step back in time with me for just a moment, to a certain winter evening more than ten years ago, when I was first learning dependence upon God's wisdom. It was well after five, and the weak winter sun had set. Darkness settled upon the wilderness except for the faint illumination of the moon. "Father, let's go cross-country skiing!" Matthew exclaimed as I lay back in the recliner.

Remember what I said earlier about the immediate problems of life tending to stomp out our dependence upon God? Well, my flesh wanted to say something like this: "What do you mean? I've already had my shower and the last thing in the world I want to do is go out and get all sweated up again skiing. I'm comfortable and I don't want to!"

"Matthew, I've already had my shower . . ." I began.

Jim, have you asked Me what you should do?

"Well, no, Lord, but . . ."

Jim, you need to go cross-country skiing with your son.

I had learned that the Christian life is about choices and I made mine. "Let's go!" I told Matthew. I wish you could have seen his face. You see, my previous comment about my shower had already told him what my choice was and he had started to turn away with the attitude of "I knew you wouldn't go." Now his face lit up and he ran to get ready.

The Christian life is one of living by principle rather than feeling, which is a good thing because my feelings were unsettled as Matthew led the way uphill. I was working and sweating, the comfort of the warm, dry cabin with my feet up in the recliner was now just a memory. "Lord, is this just to humble me?" I prayed. There was no answer.

At last we started downward and I took the lead. As we entered an area of thick evergreens the moonlight was almost fully blocked out and an oppressive darkness hung in the air. I felt impressed to stop in this eerie spot and wait for Matthew. As he drew up beside me I felt impressed to ask him the following question. "Son, if you were here right now and I wasn't with you how would you feel?"

The light was extremely bad, but even so I could see the answer on his face before he ever said it. "Thank You, Lord." I breathed. You see, I didn't know, hadn't even suspected, but Matthew's words confirmed my impression.

"Father, I would be scared to death!"

My oldest son Matthew was scared of the dark!

God knew it all along, but I didn't. Only by obeying God and going skiing with my son was I able to become aware of the problem and help him through the grace of God to overcome this fear. It wasn't exactly unknown to me. I could sympathize. I had been scared of the dark my whole life until I became a Christian.

Countless people go around like Matthew, fearful that some unknown monster is going to attack them. The Christian need not have such fears. Fear is an element of evil and when we are tempted to be fearful, we need to ask the Lord to deliver us from those feelings of fear in the same way the Christian must surrender other feelings like hurt, anger, or bitterness to the Lord.

I talked to Matthew about this and shared how I had overcome these fears. After I surrendered them to God, I looked for opportunities to confront those lies of Satan and prove them false. Matthew grasped hold of the concept and earnestly desired deliverance from these wrong feelings. Soon I saw him exercising the principles.

For example, his mother asked him to take something to the garage one evening and while he hesitated, he agreed to do it with a flashlight. On his way back to the house, he heard the voice of God prompting him with a quiet, *Why don't you try it without the flashlight?* He did, and his delight knew no bounds when he saw he could walk in the dark and not be afraid.

It took several months of lots of little incidents and practice sessions like this. Step by step, his fear of the dark was vanquished. Please don't misunderstand the point. It wasn't that Matthew overcame this fear on his own or even with our help. Rather, Matthew gained the victory through God's grace over Satan, who had been harassing him with these thoughts of fear. He learned to turn the feelings of fear over to Jesus and leave them there.

Around that same time, I had to fly from Montana to the Midwest, changing planes at Salt Lake City and then again in the Midwest. My flight was late arriving in Salt Lake City, and my connecting flight was leaving just as I arrived. It was going to be a while before I could get on another flight, so I sat down. I had prayed that the Lord would through His providence work something out so I would make my connection on time and not inconvenience those who were going to pick me up for my speaking engagement, but it appeared that this was not to be. Glancing over from my seat in the waiting area, I noticed the sign-up booth for that particular airline's frequent flyer program, and the Lord prompted me with this thought.

Go sign up for the frequent flyer program.

I don't feel like it. I missed my flight, and I don't fly this airline enough to make it worthwhile. God often does things like this. He asks us to do things that seem to our human wisdom and reasoning not to make any sense. His real reason is cloaked. In any case, I got out of my chair and headed over to the counter for I was learning to let God be all in all for me.

After telling the attendant I wanted to sign up for the frequent flyer program, she asked for my ticket. This was a little unusual, but I handed it over. "When are you going to get a flight out?" she asked. I told her what I had been told about the time for the next flight and she responded, "Sir, we've got a flight leaving right now and I can get you on it." I was not only on time for my connection; I was actually early!

Now why did God use the guise of signing me up for the frequent flyer program to help me make my fight? Think what my reaction might have been if He had said, *Jim, go to the frequent flyer desk and the attendant there will get you on an earlier flight.* You know, don't you? That's right. I would have argued with God. After all, it is ridiculous to think that the frequent flyer attendant had better flight information than the ticket counter.

God is so kind that He often saves us from ourselves by holding back from our knowledge that which might hinder us. Therefore, God sometimes asks us to do something under a pretense that we understand and will act on, when in reality, He who can see the end from the beginning is in His wisdom ordering events for our benefit.

What a wonderful God we serve! It is a shame that so few who claim to be Christians actually know Him. Astonishingly, most churches these days promote not Christ but themselves. The churches, religious schools, and colleges have built themselves into mighty bureaucratic institutions that have forgotten the very purpose of their founding.

Today, the church by and large returns converts to itself rather than to God. Funds become the lifeblood of all such empires, and all that hinders the free flow of funds is shunned. Therefore, we sit, satisfied to convince the membership they have been born again and are saved rather than teaching them to make God all in all, in their lives. It is a fearful record of neglect, which the Christian church must one day face. This building up of the institution, this linking of people to a church rather than to God was clearly rebuked by Christ's life and ministry. Christ did not oppose the Jewish church in His day but was more concerned that the individual gain a living, vibrant connection with Him rather than a membership in the church.

In many ways, today's minister has the same dilemma I had, as I stood before those realtors. Do we share the popular, expected message or do we share with our hearers that which has a chance of transforming their lives, even at the risk of unpopularity or critical comment?

I began with my presentation on good sales techniques and the relationship between buyers and sellers. Then I said, "If you follow the steps I have outlined for you this afternoon you will find success in your practice, but not the kind of success I have had. It is kind of like my son's cookie recipe. Everyone loves his cookies, and he gives the basic recipe out to anyone who asks, but when they go home and make the cookies, they complain that they just don't come out as good as his do. This is because my son uses a secret ingredient in his cookies that no one else duplicates. Friends, there is a secret ingredient to my success as a realtor as well.

"The secret is a living connection with the Lord Jesus Christ, every moment of every day. This enables me to inquire of the Lord what is the best property for my client. This enables me to put ambition and concern over my profit aside and tell some clients that this isn't the type of area they want to live in. 'I can tell your wife doesn't want to be this far from town. It is too remote.' I sometimes tell other clients that they are overextended. 'Sure the bank would probably give you the loan, but they don't care for your happiness down the road. I do. Sell your other property before you buy.'

"Friends, my secret of success is that I am not their realtor, God is! He simply allows me to act as His representative. This is the secret to success available to any of you who wish it."

Remember how I had worried and fretted so much about their reaction? Well, at least 90 percent of those present came up to me and thanked me for the presentation. They told me it brought back their childhood upbringing and more than one observed, "What are you doing selling real estate? You ought to be a preacher!" Little did I realize how prophetic their words were.

So, what about you? I know you cannot enjoy living life the way you have been. It's hard to breathe without a breathing apparatus. Do you want to try and place your dependence upon God? Will you allow Him to be your "all" and then make Him "all" in everything you do or think? He bids us, "Come unto Me all ye who labor and are heavy laden."

Come to the air. Come make Him your all. Paul says, "Put ye on the Lord Jesus Christ." He is your breathing regulator. He is the only thing that allows you to survive in this world of sin. And after you have put Him on, never let Him go!

CHAPTER 11

The Fourth Pivotal Point

"How long halt ye between two opinions? if the Lord be God, follow him: but if Baal, then follow him. And the people answered not a word" (1 Kings 18:21).

Tears poured from my eyes uncontrollably. The individual drops formed tiny rivers as they made their way down my cheeks and dropped onto the bed while other drops followed my nose until they splattered on my Bible. How long I sat this way, I'm not sure. But before long, Sally awoke and looked up at me. "Honey, why are you crying?" she asked.

Where do I begin, I wondered. *Do I start with that weekend's speaking engagement? Do I go back to the invitation? How can I explain it when Sally has unwittingly been involved from the very start?* At last I decided to start at the very best place . . . the beginning! So I took a deep breath and began to tell the story of the fourth pivotal point.

Dictionaries define "pivotal" in words like this: The thing on which something turns, the central, crucial, or critical point. That morning with Sally I had definitely come to a decision that fulfilled that description. It was in fact one of several pivotal points in my life and the fourth one of which I was aware in my relationship with God.

When I first learned of the Word of God and saw that it was more than fables and prayers, I quickly reached the first pivotal point in my relationship with the Lord. If I accepted His Word as the sole guide of my life and was serious about applying the truths it contained to my life, significant changes in the way I lived my life would take place. Was I willing to let God have that much rule in my life?

I decided that I would make those changes and accept His revealed will for my life. I found this changed the way I viewed myself and my family. I quit smoking and drinking because I saw that my body was the temple of God. Christ had died for me and purchased me at the price of His own life, therefore I was not my own, to do with as I pleased. As I learned more about the Bible, I tried to share, and my zeal—well-meaning though it was—drove a wedge of prejudice between my family and myself. The choice to try and follow God's Word dramatically altered my course of my life. Hence, my first pivotal point was accepting the Word of God as the absolute authority in my life.

My second pivotal point came when my understanding of God's Word led me to join a church different than the one in which I had been raised. Some people seem to switch denominations like most of us change shirts, but for me this was an earth-shattering step. I knew that true religion should not be taken lightly. It was a hard thing for me to realize that even though I had been raised with certain beliefs, and trained by sincere parents, these facts alone do not make a religion a practical, life-changing, life-altering force.

The third pivotal point was when God convinced me that we needed to move to the wilderness and become truly converted. This was a struggle because so many who we had thought were solid Christians opposed our plans and worked hard to convince us that we were mistaken. Now we understand beyond all doubt that we made the right choice.

It could be argued that every time you and I face a choice, we are at a pivotal point, and to some degree that is true. But the pivotal points of which I speak are the far-reaching, life-altering choices that change the course of our personal history.

When Moses sent twelve spies into the land of Canaan, ten of them chose to present a discouraging report before the people. Only two were hopeful. The nation was at a pivotal point! Their choice to turn away, to become discouraged, cost that entire generation the opportunity to enjoy the land of promise.

After several years in the wilderness, I suddenly felt myself caught up in a pivotal decision. We had found just about everything that we had gone to the wilderness to obtain. We had come to truly know God and were growing ever closer to Him. Learning to subdue self and remain surrendered to God yielded spectacular results. We moved from being married to having real MARRIAGE! The family changed into a real FAMILY! My wilderness real estate practice took off and provided a great income for our family. We were out of debt, and I was only working three days a week. The influences of the outside world were kept to a minimum, and even in conjunction with my work, we went to town no more than twice a month.

We had it made! We were living our dream!

At the moment of success, the Lord said, *Jim, I want you to put down the real estate. I want you to work for Me in a full-time ministry. The focus of that ministry will be restoring lives, restoring marriages, and restoring families.*

I remember saying to God, "Lord, I can't!" And I was right. In my own strength I couldn't minister for the Lord, but that wasn't fully what I intended. Instead, my comment revealed my real feelings. *I have life made, Lord,* I thought. *You are asking too much!*

Prior to this, I had spoken here and there as people I knew invited me. I was successful in real estate. I had an income, and my time spent preaching was just a sidelight. Now it seemed that the Lord wanted just too much of me.

As I thought about it, I struggled to decide. I looked at the life of Moses, who was in line to be king, to be Pharaoh when God asked him to leave it all behind. Then there was Peter and the other fishermen that Jesus called to follow Him. They were being asked to follow this poor and unrecognized Preacher. Those choices were pivotal points in their lives. Nothing would ever be the same no matter what they decided. And I quickly realized that this call to ministry was a pivotal point for me as well.

Dear reader, you too have pivotal issues in your life today. I don't know what God is asking of you, but you do and the Holy Spirit does.

The problem comes when God asks for something that we are not sure we want to do. Then we enter into a "standoff" with God. For some, this standoff sours and eventually kills their love for God. Everyone has at least one of these pivotal points in their life. I can say with confidence that you do as well. There is something God is asking you to deal with. He wants you to choose to go deeper with Him. I pray that the Holy Spirit will place this decision at the forefront of your thoughts as you read. I pray that God will give you no peace and no rest until you are surrendered fully to Him. I surely had no peace as I strove to come to terms with this unexpected call to ministry.

There I was in the wilderness enjoying the fruit of the lifestyle God had called us to, and I had to decide what would become of this standoff between my soul and God. The rich young ruler in the Bible had a standoff with God, and it cost him everything. Now I had to choose if I would work for God or simply be content to nuzzle the good life we had found.

If I went into ministry full time, how would I support my family? Where would the money come from? I knew the Lord could provide, but would He? Was this really what He wanted for me? Was I really willing to put myself in His hands, without knowing where the support for myself or my family was going to come from? I felt I needed some confirmation. I remembered Gideon in the Bible and how he used a fleece for confirmation of the call of God. So I kept praying, "Lord, I need a fleece for this call to the ministry, but I don't know what to ask You for."

About this time, a woman I knew called to invite me to speak at her church. "Jim," she said apologetically, "we really want you to come, but the time we have available is the Fourth of July weekend. With the holiday, there will probably be less than twenty people in attendance. We'll understand if you don't want to come for so few people."

As she spoke, the prompting of the Lord came to me saying, *This is your fleece if you want it, Jim.*

So I said, "Of course I'll come."

Then turning to God in prayer I said, "Lord, if You've really called me to speak to people full time, I want there to be people for me to speak to. I don't think that thirty or even forty people would be a miracle so I am asking You to bring fifty people—two and a half times the number she said would be there."

I was the first person at the church that day. I was motivated. I wanted to see how the Lord was going to answer my prayer. Had the Lord really called me to be a minister? Sally and I sat near the front as people came in and by the time I got up to speak, there were eight people in the church. "Well, Lord," I said to myself, "I guess I got my answer."

The door opened just then and a family of four came in. "That's still only twelve, Lord." Another three people came in. "That's fifteen." Then two more and a family of four brought the number to twenty-one. Soon it was twenty-eight, then thirty-four, and forty, and soon it was forty-three.

I was trying to preach, but inside my emotions were in turmoil. I tried to follow my sermon notes, but it wasn't easy to count and preach at the same time. I'm sure they must have wondered what was wrong with me as surely I was distracted. I kept thinking, *This can't be happening*, and yet it was.

The numbers continued to climb—forty-eight, and then fifty-one, then sixty. I was still preaching and counting, but it didn't stop. The next thing I knew, it was seventy-three and soon climbed to seventy-eight. Finally, I gave up. I cried out in my heart, "Lord, I quit counting! I have my answer!" Still the people came until the little church was full.

Well, I preached my heart out to those people. I was on fire because I knew that this was what God had called me to do. After the sermon I asked everyone I could, "Why did you come today?"

"We had no intention of coming today," one told me. "We just didn't feel like going camping as we had planned."

"I don't know," said another. "We just felt that we had to be here today."

"We had other plans," one couple shared, "but someone called us and said, 'There is this fellow coming to church this week. We heard a tape of his and it was really good! He's coming over 1,600 miles and is only going to be here one day. Change your plans; you've got to come.' So, we changed our plans and came." And so the stories went of unexpected phone calls or last minute cancellations of prior commitments. Only I knew the real reason they had come. God was speaking to me through their actions. *Jim, you asked for fifty, but I'm giving you more than fifty. I want you to work for Me!*

As I talked with those dear people on their way out of church, I thought repeatedly, *What a God I serve!*

"Lord, You're asking me to go out and be a fisher of men, and here I stand. I am not trained by any literary institution of the world, but trained up in the wilderness by Your Spirit. But Lord, what do You want me to teach them?"

Jim, I want you to teach them the practical gospel of how to walk by faith. Teach them how to abide in Me, how to live by grace, and how to apply that in their daily life—to their marriages, to their families, to their churches, and to their contacts with the world. Let them understand the basis of the gospel, which is a living experience in Me. Let them understand that this is to be their experience moment by moment, hour by hour, day by day.

And Jim, as it is recorded in Revelation 12:11 'They overcame him by the blood of the Lamb, and by the word of their testimony; and they loved not their lives unto the death.'Your preaching is not to be as the common preaching that is so popular in the churches today. You are to preach from your own personal testimony—to incorporate the power of Christ in you, the hope of glory at every opportunity. Thus the blood of the Lamb is always to be held up before the people in every sermon you give.

Jim, you are not to love this wonderful life you have found with

Me in the mountains. Rather, I want you to forsake the life you have found for the benefit of others. I am calling you to spend time away from your mountain retreat to share your testimony with others, that they too may find the practical gospel and that it may transform their lives as yours has been transformed.

I went to bed that night knowing the Lord was asking me to forsake the lucrative real estate practice with which He had so blessed me. However, when I awoke the next morning at 4:30, I sat there in bed with the Bible on my lap, shaking. The wonderful emotional experience of my answered prayer was over and now I was dealing with reality. Would I actually do it?

Finally I said, "Lord, Gideon had a second fleece. And I too, Lord, if I am to never look back at this moment, if I am never going to regret this decision, I need a second fleece. You must confirm this call to ministry in Your Word. Lord, I know I said I would work for You if You sent the people, but Gideon said he would go too with the first fleece, and still he asked for a second sign of confirmation.

"Lord, this is a tough call. I mean, this is a no-looking-back decision. This is the rest of my life. To never do another thing but this which You have asked me to do. I have never done anything like this before," I told Him. "I want You to confirm in Your Word, my calling to the gospel ministry."

Now that is a hard thing to ask, because there is no place in the Bible that says, "Jim Hohnberger, you are to become a minister of the gospel."

There I sat with my Bible. I prayed and searched my heart to make sure there was nothing between myself and God. Having done that, I started leafing through the Bible page by page for almost an hour until I came to the book of Ephesians, chapter three. It was like the Holy Spirit shook me and said, *This is the right place.*

"Lord, I feel impressed I should read here."

Start on the right column, Jim.

My eyes fell onto verse seven, "Whereof I was made a minister, according to the gift of the grace of God given unto me by the effectual working of his power."

I had shivers from my head to my toes! Wow! Talk about confirmation! Now I knew God had called me and that His grace would sustain me. I sat there in bed with the tears running down my face until Sally woke up. I told her all that had happened and how she had been a part of this, even though she had no idea at the time.

The call of God upon the heart is often unknown to those about us. You may be the only one who knows what God is asking of you at this moment. Even your spouse may not know what the pivot point in your life is, but you do. Whatever it is must be dealt with. Today as you read these lines, you are choosing—even if your choice is simply to try and put off that choice. All of us need to understand that when we decide not to make a choice, in essence, our choice has been to reject that which God is asking us to do.

"Sally," I said, "when we get home, I will no longer be in real estate. I can't sell my real estate practice because God has asked me to give it to another man."

This Christian man and his family had moved to our area from California. They didn't have much, and the man was trying to get on his feet. I could have sold that real estate practice with all its listings for tens of thousands of dollars. But God told me to give it to this other family and to commit to work with that man every week for a year, so he could give his family the same opportunity I had been given by God.

I had argued, "Lord, someone would give me fifty or sixty thousand dollars for that practice. I mean, that could be my nest egg. That's money I could use to support myself for the next couple of years while You get this ministry thing going."

But the Lord said, *No, Jim. Your dependence needs to be on Me and not a nest egg in the bank.*

So I went home and told the other family my story. They prayed about it and a week later, I started training him to sell real estate. It took about two months before he was settled and I could move on to my once-a-week commitment. By September, I was ready to ask, "Lord, what do I do? Here I am, send me."

A call came from California asking me to come and work with

five or six families who were having trouble. *This is your first call, Jim,* the Lord told me. I went gladly, and we worked with those families. I came home feeling really high because for the first time, these families came to understand the practical gospel and were starting to apply it to their lives. As they began to make even little changes, they were beginning to experience the wonderful results of living by principle and cooperating with God.

I was invited to a friend's house to talk with a man who was visiting. This man was a minister, and while I didn't know it at that time, he was soon going to be hosting a gathering of more than fifty ministers from around the world. They talked with me about the problems in the churches and what they felt the solutions could be.

I couldn't agree with them. I shared with them that the problems consisting of issues of doctrine and practice were really only symptoms of the real problem, which is that the churches have lost sight, completely lost sight of the practical gospel that is able to transform lives. I didn't expect it, but this minister told me of their upcoming meeting and asked if I would be willing to give the opening and closing address to the visiting ministers.

I will never forget the sermon I preached that day titled, "Who Am I?" I shared with those ministers that they were completely inadequate to do the work they were called to do and their need of continual dependence upon God. By the time I finished that opening address, the men were in tears, and my sermon changed the focus of the whole conference.

After this conference, calls to speak came from Europe, New Zealand, England, and all over the United States. I had wondered where the calls were going to come from. God knew. After this conference, the calls poured in as those men shared my name around the world. I can only accept a handful of the requests we receive. Since that day, we have spoken in fourteen different countries and in all but five states. Magazine articles followed and I was privileged to share the gospel on satellite television. So I set my hand to the work and have never turned away to this day.

What about you, my friends? Have you turned away? Is there

something in your life right now that God is asking for you to surrender to Him, some pivotal point where you are holding out on God? Don't put it off. Everything must inevitably be faced someday. Won't you resolve it right now?

Often I end a series of meetings by asking those attending what they are going to do with the messages they have heard. This is a deeper question than asking if they believe. Actions are always the outgrowth of true belief. My heart has been thrilled and tears have often come from my eyes as countless families have committed to making the gospel a practical reality in their lives. I ask them publicly because this public statement encourages others while at the same time it cements the decision made in their heart.

So I am asking you to write down the pivot point in your life that God is asking you to surrender to Him. Use the form below if you wish or write it down on a separate sheet of paper. In any case, choose today, for now is the hour, and never again will the Spirit's voice be louder.

My Pivot Point With God

Lord, I realize that I have had a standoff with You in the following area. I surrender it to You today!

_____

_____

Your Child,

_____

The Hesitant One

"Almost thou persuadest me" (Acts 26:28).

I knew Paul's island was supposed to be a beautiful place. Still, the sight of it made my pulse quicken with delight. The rhythmic movement of the paddles and the quiet sound of lake water dripping off the blades seemed completely in harmony with our peaceful surroundings.

Shaped somewhat like a volcano, the island rose steeply from the lake. Its foliage occasionally granted our interested gaze a glimpse of the lake home, deepening our anticipation. We had been looking forward to this trip for some time. This island was to be our vacation home until the following Monday.

My family needed this time away. The pressures of travel and ministry had motivated me to think about our need for rest and relaxation, activities that were increasingly hard to do at home. We could, and certainly did, turn off the phone when we needed a break. However, even when intentionally set aside, household jobs and ministry correspondence have a way of exerting their own pressure upon us.

Because of this, I finally approached Paul about using his island. Paul was both friend and mentor to me in my real estate practice, but I had never asked him anything like this before.

"Paul, my family is stressed out! We need a place where we can go to just rest and relax, a place where nobody knows how to reach us. Could we use your island? Oh, and Paul, while we are there, is there some type of project you need done—some type of repairs or cleanup we can do for you? That way we can be givers and not just takers."

Paul was visibly pleased. "I've never done this before," he said, "but then, no one has ever been willing to do something in return for me either. They all just want to use the island. Jim, I'd be delighted to let your family spend some time there and I'm sure we can find something for you to do while you're there."

My reminiscing ended abruptly as the canoe slid alongside the dock. After carrying our baggage up the hill to the delightful lake home, Sally and I headed back down to the dock. "Boys," I instructed, "you make the meal and when it's ready, come down to the dock and get us. We're going down to the dock to sit in the sun."

This might seem a little strange for a father to say to his ten- and twelve-year-old sons, but we had learned to turn the kitchen duties over to the boys. In far too many families, the mother is practically a servant to the children. No husband should allow such a situation to continue. The whole family must help to lift the burden of the household tasks from the mother. If this is done, the family will find that not only will the children learn important lessons of home maintenance, but they gain a mother and the husband a wife who has time and energy to play with them and share their lives.

Try lifting from your wife or from your mother any burdens that other family members can bear, and you will find your efforts more than repaid in the loving attention that she can now invest in you and the other members of her family. If the family will redeem those energies that were once consumed in everyday household tasks, everyone benefits.

I am very mindful that the wife and mother is the heart of the home, and the surest recipe for happiness in the home is for the woman who plays such a crucial role to have the energy and enthusiasm to fulfill her God-given mission.

My boys, as usual, prepared a wonderful meal. Then, with a little free time before our normal mealtime, they set off to explore the island.

Relaxing at the dock was an awfully easy thing to do in such a conducive setting. Located in a tiny inlet bay, the clear, jade waters reflected the sun until it seemed that each tiny wavelet was crowned with shining diamonds, which sparkled as they moved. Peace, contentment, and quiet conversation came naturally as we enjoyed the chance to reconnect with each other. Suddenly, the sounds of footsteps thundered down the steep stairs that lead up from the dock to the rest of the island. Matthew and Andrew raced down the stairs, chattering incessantly with all the excitement and enthusiasm only ten- and twelve-year-old boys can possess.

"Father, Mother, you've got to come see them!"

"We've got to see what?"

"Diving boards!"

Gradually through the enthusiasm, we found out from the boys that on the west side of the island were some tall cliffs. On those cliffs were some diving boards. One was about as high as a one-story house and the other was as high as a two-story house. The boys were as excited as they could be about these boards. Deep down inside they wanted to jump off those boards, but they were still young enough at that point in their lives that they wouldn't have considered any such thing unless their father lead the way.

"Can you go off them, Father?"

"Of course I can," I responded without much thought.

"Let's go!" they exclaimed.

"Wait a minute! Just hold on a minute!" I interrupted. "I think we ought to have lunch first, then maybe we can go over to the other side of the island and look at those boards."

In truth, I was hesitating. I knew I could jump off those boards. I had been off high boards before. I knew I would not get hurt. I knew that Paul had put those boards there for a reason, and without doubt many others had jumped into those waters. So there was no fear that the water wasn't deep enough. My boys wanted to see me go. I wanted to please my sons, and still I hesitated. I wasn't all that sure I wanted to go through with it.

After lunch, the boys did the dishes—in record time, I might add. They were excited. This was going to be a big adventure. They came to me and said, "Are you ready to go off those boards, Father?"

I was still hesitant, so I stalled for time. "When I was growing up," I told them, "I was always told you should wait at least an hour after eating before you swim to prevent cramps. I'll go in an hour."

Now, I must confess that I have no idea if that fact is true, and I doubt that I would have been inclined to abide by such a rule if I had wanted to go off those boards. Under the circumstances it was just an excuse, a rationalization giving me permission to avoid making a decision. My boys were disappointed at another delay, but when an hour had passed they were right back with the same question.

"Are you ready to go now, Father?"

"OK," I said. "Let's go."

They were off to the other side of the island like I had shot them out of a cannon. Sally and I walked a little slower than our enthusiastic boys. When we arrived at the diving boards, where do you think my boys were standing? By the lowest board? Not hardly! They were by the highest board. "Up here, Father!" they called.

"All right, I'm coming."

Climbing to the highest board, I walked out to the edge and looked once more at the beautiful jade waters of this gorgeous mountain lake. When you stand at the end of a diving board, it seems twice as far down to the water as it looked from below. As I stood there looking down, my boys were shouting instructions to me that went something like this:

"Jump! Jump! Jump! Why don't you jump?"

"Just give me a minute to appraise the situation. I'm going to count to ten," I told them, "and then I'm going to go off."

The boys caught hold of this idea and, seeing a way to hurry me along, began to count for me in an incredibly speedy fashion, "One, two, three, four, five, six, seven . . ."

"WHOA!" I called out to them. "I'll do my own counting. Thanks anyway."

So there I was, torn between two separate desires, two separate loves. On the one hand I loved my boys, wanted to please them, wanted to fulfill their expectations, to be their hero. But my self-will was loath to cast fear aside and take that step. So there I stood, suspended between the heavens above and the green waters below.

Intellectually, I knew others had taken the step off that board, and it was possible for me to do the same. I desired to make the jump, not only for myself, but to encourage my boys. The battle raged because I had to choose to go off the board of my own volition, that is, through the exercise of my own free will. And this is just the conflict we face when called to surrender to the will of God.

Whenever we are brought to the choice between what self-will wants and what we know God is calling us to, there is a conflict. And the common reaction to this conflict is hesitation. We know God is calling us to an experience of full surrender, and yet we hesitate. We know that others have taken that step of full dependence on Him. We know that God never fails those who trust Him, and still we hold back.

In many ways, we are like the children of Israel after leaving slavery in Egypt. They had left one life behind but had not yet entered the Promised Land. We too have a long road left to travel in our pursuit of God. Perhaps we left bad habits or bad associates behind us. Maybe doctrinal errors or traditional understandings fell by the wayside. Then again, we may have turned away from worldly entertainment, music, and fashions only to find out that, truthfully, while we may have come out of our past, we have failed to enter our future—a life hid with Christ in God (see Colossians 3:3).

Looking back at my life, I see that my journey toward this goal of full surrender has been by small increments rather than one big step. It has been this way in my life, not because God willed it that way, but because it was the manner in which I would respond. My life had often been like the verse written by Theodore Monroe:

Oh, the bitter pain and sorrow
That a time could ever be,
When I proudly said to Jesus,
"All of self and none of thee."

Yet He found me: I beheld Him
Bleeding on the accursed tree;
And my wistful heart said faintly,
"Some of self and some of thee."

Day by day His tender mercy,
Healing, helping, full and free
Brought me lower, while I whispered,
"Less of self and more of thee."

Higher than the highest heavens,
Deeper than the deepest sea,
"Lord, thy love at last has conquered;
None of self and all of thee."

I wouldn't want to give you the impression, nor would I dare say that this last step has been fully realized in my life, but I would say that I see the progression, and I am a prisoner of hope. I know that He who has begun a good work in me will continue it until the day of Jesus Christ (see Philippians 1:6).

What is God saying to you right now on your diving board? I know you are hesitating over something. Likely, it has something to do with the commitment you wrote out in the last chapter. Or perhaps it's a sensitive area God brought to your mind when you looked at the commitment form, but you were afraid to commit it to God or even to admit it was there to yourself.

You desire to surrender this sensitive area, but it's hard to believe that you'll be happy if you let it go. This is Satan's greatest lie. He has deceived all of us into believing that we can only be happy when we get our own way. Don't trust your feelings. Instead, act on principle. Your intellect must decide that feelings and emotions will no longer be allowed to control.

If you do this, you will discover that you have unlocked the secret of a happy Christian life. You will find, as I have, that the very step from which you drew back was the path to peace and happiness.

That's just what I found when I jumped off that diving board! It was great. I screamed and yelled and cheered all the way down. When I hit that refreshingly cool water, I felt more alive than ever before. I climbed out and went off the board again and again.

My son Matthew came up to me and asked tentatively, "Do you think I could go off, Father?"

"Of course you can," I answered.

So he got up on that board and went through his own hesitating process. Finally, he did it. I could see he was scared, but he held himself bravely and entered the water just as straight as an arrow.

Then Andrew came up to me and said, "Father, I want to go off that board but I'm scared. Will you go with me?"

"I sure will, Son. Give me your hand. I'll be with you all the way."

He was scared to death! I didn't push him but stood there with him while he worked through his own hesitation and then I let him count and then we jumped. I wish you could have seen the grin on that boy's face. You would have thought he had conquered the world!

Then all three of us turned to Sally. But she taught us all a lesson in bravery. "If you're going, I'm going!" And she did!

All of us learned to overcome our hesitation and gain the victory over those feelings and emotions which try to hold us back. The true Christian life is like that board. It often requires a leap of faith, a decision that we're not going to turn back, just as we couldn't get back on that board after stepping off. We were committed! This is what God is looking for in each of us.

Go ahead!

Leap out and take that last great step!

CHAPTER 13

The Last Great Step

"When all things shall be subdued unto him,
then shall the Son also himself be subject unto
him that put all things under him, that God
may be all in all" (1 Corinthians 15:28).

As I studied the rock face ahead of us, I planned the next phase of our climb. Matthew's quiet call interrupted my reverie. I glanced back down at him and realized immediately he was in trouble. We were climbing up Iceberg Peak in Glacier National Park. It was one of our father-son outings.

I take these trips with each of my sons, believing that it is important for a father to be alone with each of his children, engaged in activities they want to do. This binds our hearts together and opens the avenues of communication. Matthew had chosen this climb, and here we were, free climbing in an area that really demanded ropes and belay devices.

Matthew was stuck! He had followed my route up the mountain until he was stranded on the ledge below me. I had been tall enough to reach up to the next ledge and pull myself up, but Matthew, who was at that time still shorter than I am, couldn't reach high enough to complete this maneuver. I quickly dropped down and extended my hand to him. "Grab hold of my hand, Son. I will pull you up."

I could see the struggle on his face with fear and doubt. Can Father really do it? Does he have the strength? What will happen to me if he lets go?

"Grab my hand, Matthew! I have the strength. I can keep you from falling," I encouraged him. He glanced down. It was a long way, and his countenance demonstrated the battle that raged in his thoughts. Was he willing to take that leap of faith, trusting that I would be able to do what I had promised?

His hand reached for mine and we clasped hands. In a moment it was over, and he was standing beside me on the ledge. After a few moments to catch our breath, we resumed our assent. We climbed Iceberg Peak that day, but success would have been impossible had Matthew not chosen to take that step of absolute dependence upon his father.

This step of absolute dependence is what we are all called to. You know it in your heart-of-hearts, just as I do. You know that the Lord is calling you to this dependence and surrender, but still we hold back. We probably would have a hard time putting into words just why we pull back from this experience.

Total dependence upon God, the willingness to step out in reckless abandonment of self, is what makes the Christian life practical and forever life-changing. Dependence upon God, fully and completely, should be the very first lesson of the Christian life. Because it is only as we truly trust Christ, truly commit ourselves to Him, that we can really be called Christians. For most of us—even those of us who claim to be Christians—this remains an illusive dream, an unrealized experience.

In place of this experience, we who desire to be Christians do everything but cast our dependence upon God. With almost superhuman effort, we study doctrines and teach them to others. We engage in community outreach and evangelism. Likewise, we attend worship services, hold Vacation Bible Schools, participate in marriage enrichment seminars, and accept church offices.

We make our religion personal and take time for personal devotions and personal ministry for others. We look so good and perform so many good activities that we find it hard to comprehend—but it is nevertheless true. For we have done it all, except for the only thing that really matters. We have failed to take that last great step, the only action that would have truly transformed us on the inside, as well as in the outward actions.

The last great step to being a true Christian is a cultivated distrust of self and an equally cultivated dependence upon God. We may have all the trappings of Christianity, but even when no one else can see, we know that we do not possess the power over self that a surrendered and subdued spirit brings into the life.

Praise God, it is not too late for any of us to take that step into total dependence. It was several years into what I had thought was my Christian life when God startled me by bringing this concept forcibly to my mind. *Jim, if you are ever going to be a Christian you must take this step.*

I looked, honestly looked at what true Christianity was, and I must confess, I shrunk from it. "No, Lord, I can't do it," I prayed. "I mean, to consent to give You total control, to never think my own fleshly thoughts, to never say my own fleshly words. Why, I'll be miserable, Lord!" Can you believe I'd say that to God? Would you like to know what He said back to me?

Really, Jim? Do you think that all the angels in heaven are miserable? They have the same relationship with Me that I am calling you to have. They carry out My will and not their own and yet they remain free moral agents. They obey because they choose to, and that obedience brings them joy and happiness far beyond any pleasure your earthly thoughts or words might bring you.

"It was a foolish thought, wasn't it, Lord?"

Yes, Jim. It was from the devil. It was just those types of thoughts which led the most favored angel in all of heaven to decide to rebel against Me.

So now I faced full surrender, full dependence upon God. God was calling on me to take that last great step into true Christianity. I'll never forget the struggle with my own will. I sat home one day and read more than one hundred Bible texts. All basically said the same thing, which was that the power of God is available right now, today! I only needed to have a surrendered dependence upon God to access this power.

I didn't need more doctrinal knowledge. I didn't need more good works. I didn't need to grow up into readiness for that power. Instead, my growth as a Christian couldn't go on until I was willing to take "the last great step."

"All right Lord," I concluded, "tomorrow I'll go all the way with You in total dependence. Tomorrow morning, my life will be different. In the morning, my new life begins!"

I don't know how God does it, but I am often awake in the early morning to a sense of His presence. It is not a visible or even an audible presence. Rather, I mean that I sense His Spirit's call to my heart to wake up and commune with Him. I can't explain how God can be that personal a presence with me and at the same time be present with many, many others—but He can and He does. And if you are willing, He longs for just that type of intimate communication with you too!

That first morning of my new life, I woke up a few minutes after four in the morning. Sitting up I sensed God calling to me, reminding me of my commitment to be His today and I prayed, "Good morning, Lord!" Thus began the precious time I spent that morning with God. He wanted to prepare me for the day and my prayers continued until the sleeping head beside me looked up.

Sally asked, "What are you beaming about, dear?"

"Honey," I said, "today I go all the way with God. I'm going to fully surrender to Him and I'm going to live my life today under His control."

"You are?"

"Yes."

"Really dear, come now!" she exclaimed scornfully.

Here was the first trial of my day. My wife was mocking my commitment. Objectively, I couldn't blame her. She knew the stubborn, hot-tempered German she was married to. My past resolutions and pledges of fidelity to God had been like ropes of sand, falling apart the minute they came under stress. I had never found a power able to save me from myself. "It's all right, honey," I continued. "I've had it with on again, off again dependence on God. I've had it with partial Christianity!" And so I launched into my first day of true Christianity.

I wish there was a way I could show you a video of that day, my first day as a real Christian. But a video could never demonstrate the trials and battles fought in my thoughts; for it was in my thoughts that the victories were won. I had to decide for right in my thoughts before I could produce right actions. It would consume this entire book to share with you all that happened that day. So let me share just a couple experiences with you.

I was at my desk working when I heard my boys start into a squabble in the living room. It was the type of thing I had told my sons "a thousand times" not to become engaged in. I found myself walking quickly towards them. I felt irritation rising in my flesh. I wanted to straighten them out, right now. It is so easy for parents to fall into the trap of irritation with our children because we tell them so often not to do this or that and yet they still fall into temptation. If we could see the scene as heaven does, we might find that it is not so much the children that need reproof as the parents do.

Jim, you are not ready to deal with your children until your flesh, your feelings and emotions, are fully surrendered to Me.

I knew that the Lord was right. But it is so hard to put aside what we want to do so that we can accomplish what we know the Lord's will is for us. I retreated to the bathroom and stayed there until I knew that my flesh was surrendered and I could talk decently to my sons and give them the respect they deserve.

"Boys," I said to my sons, "when I wanted to come over here and talk to you about your actions the Lord spoke to me telling me what I should do. Now, I'm sure that before you got into this disagreement, you heard the still, small voice of God calling to your conscience, telling you what to do. All of us must learn to become sensitive to that quiet voice of God and train ourselves to be quick to obey it. Your father will not always be there your whole life to guide and correct you, but your heavenly Father will guide you throughout your life if you are willing to listen. Please. Please. Please don't train your minds to reject God's guidance."

I left my time with the boys profoundly grateful that I had chosen to surrender my will to God's. My interaction with them had been that of teaching and training rather than scolding them for their misdeeds. I had approached discipline in a surrendered state and my sons could tell the difference and had a different reaction to me than in my past attempts at instruction.

Later in the afternoon, after our midday meal, I felt impressed that I should do the dishes. Now, the dishes were not my job; they were my sons' job. But I had promised the Lord that whatever He wanted me to do today I would do. "Sure, Lord," I responded in my thoughts. "If You want me to do the dishes, I will be happy to."

I gathered my plate and silverware and walked over to the sink where I got out the dishpan and started the hot water running. Now, it took my boys only two seconds to realize what I was doing. Sensing their opportunity, they quickly and willingly cleared the table, stacked the dishes for me and then vanished.

So there I stood washing the dishes enjoying my day with the Lord. Sally, however, did the strangest thing I think I have ever seen her do.

My wife never rests. We have trouble getting her to stop working in the evening to spend time with us. Not so today. She sat down in the recliner and just watched me do the dishes.

So that you will understand what follows, perhaps a word of explanation is in order at this point. The wilderness lifestyle we live brings with it many changes, and cooking on a wood cookstove is one of them. Now, I am a big fan of wood cooking. Food cooked over wood just seems to taste better. However, heat control is not an exact science.

For this particular meal, Sally had placed some items in the warming oven, including a quart jar of applesauce. The now empty jar was in the dishwater. As I started washing the jar, I noted some applesauce that had gotten baked on in the warming oven. It was on the exterior of the jar, so I half-heartedly scrubbed at the baked-on food. It was really stuck on there, like armor plating.

Now, Sally and I have always done dishes a little differently. I do them to get them done, and Sally does them to get them done right. I say that not to excuse myself but to explain that this is an area of weakness in my character. This trait allowed me to rationalize, "I don't need to spend all day on this baked-on mess. After all, the inside of the jar is clean, and that is what matters." With that thought, I rinsed the jar and set it on the drying rack.

Sally suddenly rose to her feet at this point as if propelled upward by some giant springs. Walking over beside me, she zeroed right in on that jar. She picked it up and held it up to the light right in front of my face! I couldn't believe it. It was almost as if my mild-mannered wife was intentionally provoking me! My feelings were in an uproar.

"Jim, Jim, Jim, will you ever learn?" Sally clucked, shaking her head.

In the past we had fought over the way I did dishes. I would always say, "At least I'm doing the dishes—you shouldn't complain about how I do them." Every fiber of my being wanted to let go and say exactly that sort of thing again, but I had made a commitment to be God's man today, and He was calling me to surrender my feelings to Him. I chose to give up my feelings, and once more I had peace.

It all happens in just fractions of seconds. The next thing I knew, the wet jar slipped from Sally's grasp and fell squarely in the dishpan. It covered me in a tidal wave of water and suds. I could feel the anger mounting. My flesh was dying to let her have it. That is the way we humans are without God in control of our lives. We are very quick to lash out and defend our rights and our feelings. I am so thankful that God had not abandoned me, for as soon as the feelings rose from my flesh, the God of all flesh was there by my side asking me to surrender it to Him.

It seemed so hard at the time to put those upset feelings away, really put them away, not just hold them in until the next time. God not only wanted me to surrender them, He wanted me to give up my right to ever pull them back out the next time Sally did something that upset me. God does a thorough work in our lives, and if we let Him, He will completely remove from us that which we surrender to Him.

Plucking the jar from the water, I cheerfully told Sally, "You're right. It looks like it needs a little more attention." The victory was mine through the grace of God.

Sally looked at me in shock. She knew beyond a shadow of a doubt how the hot-tempered man she loved would respond, and he didn't. "It works!" she blurted out.

"Yes, it does," I said as I smiled at her, remembering our morning's conversation and her doubts.

"How often does God speak to you?" she questioned.

"I don't know," I responded. "I don't sit there keeping track with a calculator." The next day I kept track for Sally. At 10 A.M., I went to her and said, "So far today, I am aware of eighteen times the Lord has called to me to surrender my thoughts to Him. Now I'm going to stop counting."

This last great step requires a full surrender to God, a willingness to go all the way. Christ illustrated it well in the parable of the pearl of great price. To acquire the pearl took all that the man possessed. To acquire Christ as a truly vibrant part of our life will also require a sacrifice of all that we are to be put in His control. It is a daring, all or nothing leap of faith, trusting God only.

It is very much like that leap we took from the high dive in the previous chapter. Once we stepped from that board, there was no going back on that choice. You are committed. The rite of circumcision was to teach the same lesson. Once that step was taken, there was no going back.

That afternoon I planned to cut my last load of firewood for the year. I have shared before that I like to cut firewood, so this really isn't a job I dread. I was however, unprepared for the impression that the Lord gave me when I was about halfway through loading wood in my utility trailer. *Jim, I want you to deliver this load of wood to Mitch.*

Mitch was a friend of mine who lived in another valley. I like

Mitch, but the idea of bringing him a load of wood had never occurred to me. Mitch was quite capable of cutting his own wood. He wasn't laid up in bed. Besides, it was a long way to Mitch's place this late in the day. It would require a three-hour round trip, not counting the time spent unloading the trailer. "Lord? Take a load of wood to Mitch?"

Yes, Jim. It will encourage him.

I hate to admit it, but I struggled with surrendering my plans and my way—what I wanted—and choosing God's will for me in order to do a kind deed. At length, I decided to obey and filled the trailer and prepared to head over to Mitch's house.

Jim, said that familiar voice, *when you load wood in the trailer for yourself, how do you load it?*

I looked at the trailer. It contained a nice load of wood, well-packed, loaded level with the sides. I knew instantly what God was asking of me. When I loaded the trailer for myself, I loaded it until there was a mound of wood heaped up that wouldn't hold another piece. "I understand, Lord," I prayed. "You want me to treat my brother exactly like I would treat myself, don't You, Lord?"

So I got out the chain saw and cut more wood, split, and then stacked it in the trailer until it was positively heaping. Then I called my friend to see if he would be home. One of his children informed me that they would not be home. "Can I give him a message?" she asked.

"No, no, that's quite all right. Don't even tell him I called." I assured the child. "Well, I guess that's it, Lord. I mean, he is not going to be there to receive it. No one is going to be there to help me unload or praise my efforts and tell me what a good Christian I am."

Jim, I want you to go anyway.

"But, Lord—"

That's right, Jim, I want you to go when there is nothing in it for you. When everything involved crosses your flesh. I want you to do My will, trusting that I know best.

So I drove ninety minutes to my friend's house, and, just like his daughter had warned me, there was no one home. I unloaded the wood myself and stacked it. On my way home, I ran into Mitch and his family. We pulled alongside each other and rolled down our windows. The very first words out of his mouth were, "What are you doing over here, Jim?"

My flesh wanted so badly to get a few pats on the back, and the desire rose within me to say, "I just delivered you a load of wood." However, there was also the voice of my God, my Father, Abba, my Papa God, as the Bible refers to Him, and with the tender firmness of a Father, He said, *Jim . . . .*

The true Christian life is all about surrender, and that is what I chose. "I'm just on my way home," I said quickly, truthfully, and I hoped naturally.

"Good to see you," he said as we separated.

Once I shared this message in a church in Dallas, Texas. I encouraged the people to take this "last great step" into the surrendered life in Christ, when a most unusual thing happened. I had just finished my message and sat down. The church's pastor was walking up to the podium to announce the closing hymn and to give the closing prayer when suddenly a man rose slowly from his seat and began a pilgrimage down the center aisle of the church. The pastor stood in the pulpit, speechless, and total silence reigned in the congregation. The young man knelt by the altar with graceful simplicity and quietly bowed his head.

I could tell from the way he was dressed that this young man was not a member of that church. In fact, he looked as if he had just walked in off the street. His arms were scarred and his face terribly disfigured. The pastor came to his senses and realized that this poor young man was dedicating himself to do exactly what I had just asked the congregation to do—take The Last Great Step. He was going to make the commitment. You could feel the Spirit of God striving with the hearts of the people as the pastor's beautiful voice rose in song.

> All to Jesus I surrender,
> All to Him I freely give;
> I will ever love and trust Him,

In His presence daily live;

All to Jesus I surrender;
Humbly at His feet I bow,
Worldly pleasures all forsaken;
Take me Jesus, take me now;

All to Jesus I surrender;
Make me, Savior, wholly thine;
Let me feel the Holy Spirit,
Truly know that thou art mine;

All to Jesus I surrender;
Now I feel that sacred flame.
O the joy of full salvation!
Glory, glory to His name.

I surrender all, I surrender all
All to Thee my blessed Savior,
I surrender all.

It was totally spontaneous. No call had been made, not a word spoken, no emotional appeal, and yet the Holy Spirit spoke louder than any human voice could and nearly one third of those present came forward and knelt beside that young man. Chills ran up and down my spine. I knew I had to talk to that young man and learn his story.

I took him aside to visit with him. I learned his name was "Christopher." In the slow, slurred speech of one handicapped with a speech impediment, he hesitantly told me his story. He told how his mother punished him with boiling water as a child. The burn scars on his exposed skin bore mute testimony to the truth of his story. In a few deliberate words he continued, "Sometimes she would lock me in the closet for a day or two days. When she let me out, she would have my brothers beat me with sticks. By the time I was a teenager, I couldn't stand it any more. I moved out and joined the street gangs."

I had always wondered what motivated young people to join the gangs. Now Christopher explained it to me. In the gang he found—for the first time in his tormented life—full acceptance, and " 'til death do us part" loyalty. The gangs, unfortunately, were no less violent than his previous home.

"I've been stabbed twice, and I was shot once," he stated simply. "I was also in prison. After I got out, I met these people from this church who told me about this Jesus. They told me I could trust Him like I've never trusted anyone in my life. I was interested, more than I wanted to admit, but I was also scared. Everyone I had trusted had always let me down. So I told them 'If this Jesus ever lies to me, I'll kill Him!' But they assured me He never lies. Then they told me about these meetings you were having, for people to learn how to walk with Jesus. Mr. Hohnberger, what you have talked about this weekend—letting Jesus have complete control of your life—is that what it means to be a Christian?"

"Yes it is, Christopher."

"Then I want to be a Christian."

I tried to get an address from Christopher, so I could keep in touch, but he refused. I pressed him for a phone number, but he resisted. "How am I going to stay in contact with you?" I finally asked.

"Well," he began, "I live under a bridge."

I felt the sting of his comment. I had preached to a church full of people who had every advantage and yet it was this young man who was the first to dedicate his life to Christ. I have never known anyone who had come from such rough circumstances as Christopher, yet he found no excuse in his background or his present condition to keep him from taking that "last great step" into a surrendered relationship with God.

And we, who sit in great light and blessing, refuse to heed God's call of mercy. How could I hesitate? I was so ashamed of my stubborn pride.

Looking at Christopher's example, is there any excuse we can give to God for not taking that last great step? I know you want this experience. I know you desire it. I also know that God is calling you to make a decision. Desiring is not enough; you must decide to do it. You must take that last great step.

Can you sense the frustrations God must experience as He watches us hesitate, then finally turn away into darkness, seemingly unable to tell the difference between life and death?

Listen to His words, appealing to you and to me to take that last great step: "I have set before you life and death, blessing and cursing: therefore choose life, that both thou and thy seed may live" (Deuteronomy 30:19) and escape to God.

Epilogue

Almost seventeen years have passed since we moved our family to the wilderness. Our little boys became big boys and then teenagers, until today, they stand in the fullness of manhood. Now the perspective of time permits me to look back at the last two decades of my life that are the focus of this book. From the time we announced our plans for moving to the wilderness, there were those who said it wasn't practical. When we stated that our goal was to provide our boys with the best and guard them from all the rest, they informed us that it was impossible. Our sights were set too high, they said. It can't be done!

With the passage of time I can tell you conclusively, it can be done! It does work! The program we set out on to find God and to draw together as a family absolutely works! I am not recommending anything that hasn't worked for us. Over and over people have said, "Just wait 'til your boys are teenagers. Then they'll rebel against your lifestyle."

Later, when people saw the teen years slipping by without rebellion, they changed their chant to, "Wait until they are adults."

Today, they are adults, and we no longer even notice the voices of the naysayers because we know that what we did works. And it will work for you as well, whether you live in the wilderness or just want to move to the country to apply the same principles now.

Today, Matthew and Andrew are successful real estate brokers, specializing in wilderness and country properties. Their characters, which were formed so painstakingly in the wilderness, have drawn the attention of many of their clients, and more than one have contacted me wanting to know how in the world we managed to raise such outstanding young men. The secret is simple. Sally and I didn't raise them. We allowed God to do so through our cooperation with Him. Therefore, while we rejoice with the boys in their successes, we are continually humbled by the knowledge that it has only been through the grace of God that our family has achieved such results.

At the time of this writing, the four of us continue to reside in our little log home near Glacier National Park. The boys run their real estate practices out of the home as well as maintain an office in town. They still enjoy their parents' company. If anything, our communion today is sweeter because we all know our time together will end one day. All too soon, the boys will marry and form their own homes. We have no regrets. They are ready, and so are we. Sally, my queen, and I stand ready to encourage them through each stage of life that we are privileged to witness. Until then, we cherish our time.

After the Lord called me to full-time ministry, we founded Restoration International with another family who was determined to follow God to the utmost. This nonprofit ministry is committed to teaching others how to find and live the practical gospel, so that it can transform and restore their marriages and their families, just like it did ours. We truly believe that the very essence of the gospel of Christ is restoration.

So, what of the future? Have we achieved all we set out to accomplish in possessing a marriage that is second to none and learning to walk with God? Yes, and we have realized our goal of raising our boys as true Christians.

But that is only a hint of the future. As a teen, Matthew was struck with the notion of finding a hidden lake way back in the Canadian wilderness. It became his dream, his goal, and stayed with him for years. Eventually, he achieved his goal, and by the time we returned to civilization he had already thought of new areas to explore, new adventures to be experienced.

This is how Sally and I view our future. The completion of one dream does not dim the vision of the next. Climbing one mountain only reveals more and still greater heights to conquer. Within us burns the desire to see what lies beyond the next hill. The experience of the Christian life is ever upward. There will ever be new heights of selflessness and new depths of dying to self to be explored. Each new experience brings with it increased duties and greater joys in the company of Christ, our constant Companion.

That you too, may be drawn to escape to God and press ever higher with Him is my wish, my prayer, and my heart's desire. Amen.

Hohnberger's 960 square foot log home.

Matthew feeding a pet golden mantle squirrel.

Andrew feeding Lonesome an apple.

Andrew feeding a small buck in velvet.

Lonesome licking off a plate of honey.

A Conversation With
Jim Hohnberger

Q: When you first recognized that something was wrong in your spiritual experience, what was it that led you to decide that simplifying your life was the answer?

Hohnberger: I wasn't raised in the faith that I am presently in. After we had come into the remnant church of God, we became very active in sharing the truths that brought us into the church. But I began to find out that a lot of my Christian experience was outward—church attendance, giving Bible studies, etc. I became the head elder at the church. I was preaching and had been involved a little over three years. Well, I came home one night and Sally and I got into a real bad fight. My 3-year-old and my 5-year-old were screaming. They didn't know what was going on, they were too young to under-stand. Sally went for a walk on our 40 acres, and when she came back I just said to her, "Honey, what's going on?"

Later, I called my office. (I owned an insurance agency then.) I told my office staff that I was leaving for 10 days for some time out. Sally and I pulled our travel trailer up to Imp Lake in the Upper Peninsula of Michigan by Watersmead, and spent 10 days re-evaluating our lives.

When we courted each other we were madly in love. I mean we had a beautiful romance. But once we got married we just jumped on the merry-go-round that's in this society, this giant treadmill. We thought to be happy we had to have the bigger home—We went through three homes. We were now in a 3,000 square foot, all cedar log home on 40 park-like acres with a little lake. Had all the fine vehicles; was making a great income. I was head elder of the church, very active in the community, but we had grown apart. There was an eroding process that actually separated us, and the only thing we didn't have now was each other. We had all the trappings of what "they" said was success, but we were failing.

So as we re-evaluated ourselves over those ten days, we began to look at others in my career. We looked at others in the church, not from a critical standpoint, not pointing fingers, but seeing what we could learn from them, and we didn't like what we saw. We determined that success was not in the direction that we were going. We had to regain our time (the only thing we didn't have now was time), and apply it to really finding a walk with God, not just truth, and not just the church. And then making our marriage a priority and our children a priority. And so we knew we had to get off this fast pace, this treadmill that we're on in the United States. Of course, Europe is on it, Australia, Canada and England too—it's not just the United States.

Q: Most people who are on the fast track don't even live the lifestyle you just described. They're living in sub-divisions, the suburbs, or in the city with postage-stamp sized lawns. Even though you say you had to get off the treadmill, your situation seemed somewhat idyllic, with this beautiful log home on its own private 40 acres. It sounds to me a lot more relaxing than what most people contend with when they're living in the city and working 50-80 hours a week.

Hohnberger: A lot of people have said to me, "Well, does everyone have to move to the wilderness to gain this?" And my response, especially looking back after 18 years, is that I believe that everyone needs a wilderness experience, but you don't have to go to the wilderness to gain it. You must learn how to control what is coming into your life. Whether that's in a flat in Chicago, or you're in the Bronx in New York, or you're in a country setting. I've watched a lot of people try and follow a method, and they move to the country and actually make their lives worse than before. They, like us, actually bring the city lifestyle to the country.

Q: At one point you talk about your early morning devotions and you talk about having 2 1/2 hours with God. Some people will say that's fine for you because you live in the wilderness, but what about the rest of us who live in L.A. or Toronto or Indianapolis? What kind of devotional experience can we expect to have?

Hohnberger: Well let me respond. We've been active in this ministry, Restoration International, for eight years, and the biggest mistake people make is following methods. The method you follow is that of getting out of the driver's seat—letting God be in charge.

Q: That's the main method?

Hohnberger: That is the method. And what people do is they hear what you did to you raise your children, or how you communicate with your wife, or your move to the country and they try to duplicate that. And it doesn't work for them. And the reason is because they are still in charge.

See, the whole controversy that God has with his people is that they are in charge. That's the whole issue with humanity. When Lucifer wanted to be in charge, that was the problem, and so, I can't stress enough to the people that moving to the wilderness isn't going to do it for you. Because there are many natives in Africa that are much more in the wilderness than Hohnberger is. Yet they are not under the influence of the Spirit of God. Setting can help, and we can all benefit by living in a quiet, serene setting, but people try to make the setting the answer, and it's only a tool.

The method is simple: Jim Hohnberger must learn how to surrender the control of himself in the present, and then maintain that surrender through the influence of the Spirit in his conscience, allowing God to be in control throughout the day. That is the Christian life in a nutshell.

Q: And the 2 1/2 hours?

Hohnberger: Tithing my time is what I call it. Now most people are not going to have that kind of time. That's reality and I have to deal with reality. But when I sold everything, and moved up there [Montana], I had that kind of time. So, I had a situation that was unlike the majority. And I said to God, I'm going to devote this time to you. But the idea is not the length of time, it's what you get accomplished in the time you give. That's what I like to stress. Just like a tight-rope walker, when he first has to learn how to walk across a tight-rope, it may take him days, but when he's learned how to walk it, he can do it in minutes. And this is true to a degree with our walk with God. The issue isn't the length of time or how much you read, it's whether you surrender to the Lordship of Jesus, where you realize He is in control, and you go out of that time with the Lord ready to filter your thoughts, your words, and the things you do that day, through Jesus. Now, if you can accomplish that in a half an hour, you've done it. If it takes 3 1/2 or 4 hours, take it. If you can accomplish it in 15 minutes, take it.

Q: So what you're saying is that if self is in control, the amount of time you pray and study is of no value?

Hohnberger: I'm glad you bring this up because some people think that if they put in their 2 1/2 hours, or whatever, then they're Christians. And that isn't true. Because they can be in charge of the whole program in the 2 1/2 hours. Does that makes sense? I know many men who have become scholars of the Bible, and they come out of their 3, 4, 5 hours with the Lord and treat their wives like dirt. Christianity goes beyond a mere mental assent to truth and involves the surrender of one's choices to the present will of Jesus Christ.

Q: Your ministry takes you into all areas of the church— both the liberal camps and conservative. How do you minister effectively to the various "camps"?

Hohnberger: If I can use some labels here, the conservatives jump at the more liberal members because their theology isn't quite the same as theirs, but they are mostly self-directed. And the liberals jump at the conservatives because they're critical and haughty, and puffed up. And the liberals are mostly self-directed. And God is saying, "Listen, you conservatives and liberals. You've both got the same problem. I want you to be Spirit-directed."

We've been welcomed into the various camps because our desire is to save people from themselves, not from the offshoot groups, or the conservatives, or separatists, nor from the GC. Those aren't the enemy. The enemy is in our own hearts. What good does it do to tell everybody about the beast overseas, on the seven hills, if the beast is still ruling in your own heart? So when we go into these conservative groups and they are putting up these signs about the beast and the beast power, I say to them "Can I have your wife come up here and ask her if the beast in your own heart is still ruling at home? If it is, tear down your billboards. Forget picking on the beast of Revelation and 666, and learn to deal with the beast in your own heart!"

Thus the message we have been giving has broken through the political barriers that presently exist.

Q: Are there groups you won't minister to?

Hohnberger: I believe that if we have the gospel, we are to take it to those that don't have it. As the conference presidents have called me and said, "I see that you are speaking at this particular ministry. We would ask you that you don't go there." And I say, "Do you think I have the gospel?" and they say "Yes we do." "Well how are they going to get it?" Because, if you really possess the gospel you will find a way to bring it into those people's experience, and not just throw them out.

At one of our family camp meetings, we had 550 people there, 100 of them were not of our faith. It was advertised on a billboard, on the county highway, and in newspaper ads. And some women [from the community] were coming to the meetings in cut-off shorts and tank tops, with low necklines. Well, a group of ultra-conservative people approached me in very conservative dress and they said, "Brother Hohnberger, we want you to announce a dress standard at this camp meeting." "Why?" I said. And they said "Well, you see that lady over there?" And I said "Yes, I see her." "That's why. She's defrauding us." And I said, "I just want you gentlemen to understand where I am coming from. I will try to make this as simple as I can. If she came in her swimming suit she is welcome in my meetings. Because I am after her heart, not her attire. And if we get her heart connected with Jesus' heart, the rest will be taken care of." That has been my philosophy.

Q: This book was written in an unusual setting, wasn't it?

Hohnberger: I went to the island of St. Croix for a month to write it. I am not a writer. English was something they tortured me with all the way through school. My mother said that I had to pay attention, but I said, "Mom, I'm never going to use that stuff." Well, little did I know.

I tried to write this book and I'd start it and drop it and I'd lose the flow, you know? Finally I said, "Lord, I need some uninterrupted time. Can you provide it?" So, a man my son had sold some real estate to—a fairly wealthy man not of our denomination—called me on the phone. He said, "Your son. What did you do to raise him? I have not met men in the business world like this, and your son is only 21 years old. Can I come and stay with you?" This guy owns his own bank, his own mortgage company, and he's got warehouses, and property in numerous locations. He happened to own this villa on St. Croix on the northwest side—up where the scuba diving is really good.

So he got to talking to me, and he was asking about some of my burdens, and I said, "Well you know I've been trying to write this book." And he said, "Listen, if you need some uninterrupted time, why don't you go use my villa?" "Where is it?" I asked. He replies, "St. Croix." And then the Lord provided free airfare for myself and my family. So we went there for a month. And I wrote all morning, every morning and then we went scuba diving in the afternoon.

Q: Praise the Lord. What a way to write a book!

Hohnberger: You wouldn't believe this. I'm diving at 130 feet, and you know what my mind is doing? You can't just turn it off when the brain is turned on and the flow is coming. I'm down there and I can see a shark and my mind is writing chapter 7. I'm diving through all this beauty and my brain is still writing this book.

Q: Jim, you have sermon series on cassette tape and a quarterly newsletter as well. Where can people write to order your ministry materials?

Hohnberger: Restoration International, 14000 Northfork Rd., Polebridge, MT 59928. (406) 756-4440. They can also order these materials online at our new Web site: www.restoration-international.org.

Q: Final question. What would you say, Jim, is the greatest single lesson you've learned through your wilderness experience?

Hohnberger: Wow. I need Jesus every moment of every hour of every day. And if I for a moment let go of Him, I fall back into the old ways. I would parallel it to—and I don't know if you've ever rappelled. But you simply throw a well-anchored, good rope over the side of a cliff and as long as you're holding onto that rope you're safe. If you let go, what happens? That's the same as it is in the Christian life. I've come to understand that Christianity is more than just belonging to the right church and living the right lifestyle, or living in the wilderness, or knowing about the beast and bears of Daniel and Revelation, the prophecies and second coming. What Christianity is about is holding onto that rope, which is Jesus. And I can rappel safely through this world as long as I continue to hold onto Jesus. My prayer is that I will come to such a place in my Christian life that I never choose to let go.